'Why are you going there?'

# 'Why are you going there?'

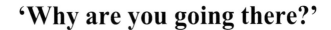

*Stories of an English teacher in Russia*

Elliot Miles Emery

# About the author

Elliot Miles Emery is the author of *'Why are you going there?'*. He graduated with a upper second class degree in Law (LL.B. Law) at the University of Birmingham before going on to graduate with a distinction in his Master's degree in Human Rights Law (LL.M. Human Rights Law) at the University of Nottingham. For almost three years he worked as an immigration lawyer in the UK representing asylum seekers. He moved to Moscow in January 2019 where he currently lives and works as an English teacher.

# Contents

# Prologue

## *'Why are you going there?'*

*The sleepy Derbyshire village where I lived,*
*prior to moving to Moscow.*

## 'WHY ARE YOU GOING THERE?'

'I think I speak for everyone Elliot when I say that you will be missed', announced my soon to be former manager of the law firm where I had been working for the past two years. Although brief, I thought that this was a lovely send off until he hastened to add 'especially when you get arrested by the KGB!' and chuckled to himself. I contemplated reminding him that in fact the KGB had ceased operating after the fall of the Soviet Union and that if I was to be arrested it would be by the much more humane organisation that is the FSB. However, he seemed particularly pleased with this joke and so I decided to let him have this one. After all, this was my final work Christmas party. Also, as he swayed there in front of me in an increasingly drunken stupor I decided that he perhaps lacked capacity to have a discussion about the intricacies of the collapse of the Soviet Union in 1991 and its aftermath at this precise moment.

On the note of sobriety, I should add that he was far from being the only drunk person in the room. In fact, everyone (apart from me and another colleague) was in varying states of drunkenness. Usually I would be right there with them. Indeed, the presence of alcohol is normally a prerequisite for me attending a work Christmas party in the first place. I find that it numbs the pain of forced joviality which surrounds Christmas. However, this year the party took place at a stately home which was miles away from where I lived and so I decided to drive. I didn't fancy paying upwards of £50 for a taxi home just so I could drink and spend several more hours listening to jokes about my impending arrest and/or death. I doubt that the consumption of alcohol would have made these jokes any funnier.

As my colleagues swayed into a nearby room with a dance floor, I decided that it was time to make my exit. As if the prospect of me awkwardly dancing for another hour like I was having some kind of seizure wasn't enough, I then heard the DJ enthusiastically booming out Abba. That was confirmation that it was time to leave. I am certainly no 'dancing queen'. I bid farewell to my drunken colleagues and headed home, leaving what would be my final Christmas party.

Just over a month earlier, I had decided to resign from my job as an immigration lawyer to start a new career as an English teacher in Moscow. I had been learning Russian for around two years and had a bizarre fascination with the country which I think stemmed from my History lessons at school. However, I had never visited Russia nor lived abroad. Nevertheless, I had been working incredibly long hours at a law firm for several years and was ready for a change.

## 'WHY ARE YOU GOING THERE?'

I enjoyed my work. I represented asylum seekers (predominantly unaccompanied children) in their asylum claims which was a worthy and important cause about which I was (and still am) incredibly passionate. However, it was also very stressful and, as with most worthy causes, not particularly well paid. In addition, I was tired of attending three plus hour interviews at the Home Office where my clients were interrogated as to why they couldn't remember the exact time of day they fled their war torn country. The fact that they couldn't remember this one detail inevitably meant that their whole case was fabricated. These questions usually came from an apathetic interviewer who was not only too lazy to read my client's fifteen page witness statement which had been submitted weeks beforehand but also to iron his own shirt.

So, in light of the above, after accepting a job offer in Moscow, I was understandably excited. However, not everyone shared this excitement. Once news of my resignation reached my manager he came over to me and asked 'Why are you going there? It's dangerous!' In fact, he was not the only person who didn't share my excitement. In the weeks leading up to my departure I noticed three different types of reactions to my news. Upon hearing my news, one group of people would look at me with pity in their eyes as if I had told them that I had just been diagnosed with a terminal illness. The second group of people would usually stare at me with a look of genuine fear in their eyes like I had just told them that I was about to jump in front of a train. The third and final (and perhaps my favourite group) reacted with a bizarre sense of anger and confusion as though I had told them that I was a spy.

Perhaps this final reaction was inspired by recent events in the news concerning the Novichok poisonings in Salisbury. I kindly reminded these people that I had had no involvement in this. However, the people whose opinions mattered to me most (friends and family) all supported my decision even if they didn't fully understand it. In any event, nothing would change my mind. I had already resigned from my current job and accepted a position as an English teacher in Moscow. I was going to Russia.

However, what I hadn't anticipated before making this decision was how exhausting it would be to pack up my life and move abroad. I was twenty seven years old and lived alone in a small rented terraced house in a Derbyshire village. I consider myself somewhat of a minimalist so I thought it would be easy to pack up my life. How wrong I was. The final few hours in my house consisted of me lying on the floor in a delirious trance begging for mercy, surrounded by nothing but bare damp walls.

## 'WHY ARE YOU GOING THERE?'

When I had moved into the house the previous year it was completely unfurnished (not even white goods). At the time I thought this was great as I could put my own 'stamp' on the place and spend hours at IKEA guzzling Swedish meatballs. What I hadn't thought about was that, when leaving the house, I would also need to get rid of all this furniture. The final days prior to my departure led to me literally throwing furniture at charity shop doors or at anyone who would have them.

As if I didn't have enough on my plate, the month before, my letting agency had announced that the landlord wished to sell the property so they would be conducting viewings. What I learnt from these viewings, as well as from trying to sell my furniture at the same time, is that people are generally excellent at asking stupid questions. I remember one lady who was viewing the house whispering to me as the estate agent momentarily left the room 'what are the neighbours like?' as if I might have some shocking, secret information. I considered telling her that on the left-hand side lived a drug dealer who specialised in Class A drugs which he would sell from behind the back of the local Co-op supermarket and that on the right-hand side there was a brothel. However, given my lack of energy, I simply muttered 'fine'. I could understand if she was viewing a property in the Bronx. However, she was viewing a property in a sleepy Derbyshire village where the average age of the population is seventy years old. The house where I lived was called 'Bluebell Cottage'. This is hardly a name which evokes images of organised crime.

On another occasion, a prospective buyer asked me what the loft was like. 'Sorry, Dave (not his real name), I have no idea', I replied as I was frantically disassembling an IKEA dining table so that someone could come and collect it for the princely sum of £10. I used various websites in an effort to sell some of my furniture/items which had been bought less than a year ago. This inevitably led to more stupid questions. One item I was trying to get rid of was a rather large plasma television. Now, I don't mind answering simple and logical questions such as 'does this television have inbuilt free view?' However, when Sandra wanted to know the day the television was built and the name of the person who built it (as well as the names of his wife and kids), I lost my patience. In the end, my television remained unsold and currently resides in my mother's garage. Another item I was trying to sell online was a sofa. One potential buyer wanted a few more pictures of the sofa (the multiple photos already online were apparently not enough), including a close up. I found myself on my hands and knees taking photographs as if I was a sleazy photographer doing a shoot for page 3 of 'The Sun'.

The night before I left I spent at my mother's house packing. I was exhausted but excited. I was excited to move to a country where I hopefully wouldn't have to answer any more stupid questions or throw furniture at random passers-by in the street in an attempt to get rid of it. I was ready to move to Russia. All I had to worry about now was my impending arrest and death at the hands of the FSB upon arrival. After the stress of the past few months, that felt like a welcome relief.

# I.

# Arrival

## *Flying, Falling and Food*

*My new home in Moscow.*

## 'WHY ARE YOU GOING THERE?'

### *Finding my new home*

It was finally here. Today was the day that I was moving to Moscow. The stress and exhaustion of the previous few months now gave way to slight trepidation as I realised the significance of the move. As I sat on the plane, ready to embark on a new chapter in my life, you might have expected me to be pondering big philosophical questions such as the meaning of life or new beginnings.

However, in fact, the only question running through my mind at this particular moment was 'What the hell is that?' as I looked down at what I presumed was my lunch. Now, don't get me wrong, I had not expected luxury. It is safe to say that, globally, plane food does not have a particularly good reputation, regardless of the airline. However, I had at least hoped that I would be able to identify the contents of my 'lunch' within a few minutes. Alas, as the minutes passed by, I was still no closer to deciphering what was before me.

As a general rule, I think that if you cannot determine the contents of a meal within the first few minutes it is probably best to assume it is inedible. However, I was hungry and so I flouted this rule. I am pleased to report that the meal tasted better than it looked and I lived to tell the tale. I did decide to give the festive (I was travelling during the New

17

Year period) chocolate bar a miss though. I have a nut allergy and, whilst I know the Russian word for nuts, I was not confident enough in my ability to say in Russian 'Help, I think I might be dying', particularly as my throat was closing up.

Around four hours later we finally touched down at Sheremetyevo airport in Moscow on what was a very cold (around -15 degrees Celsius) Saturday night. Aside from the lunch debacle, the flight had been fine. I had decided to fly with the national Russian airline which was considerably cheaper than its British counterpart. A former colleague had joked that I would need to bring my own seatbelt but luckily this was in fact included in the price. So, all in all, I had no complaints. However, I would add that, generally, I am easily pleased. If I do not die I consider the flight to have been a success.

After disembarking, I headed inside to collect my baggage and find my new manager who was meeting me at the airport. After around half an hour I finally had all my baggage and met my new manager. He greeted me with a warm handshake and smile and we headed outside to get a taxi which would take me to my new home. Other than the fact that I would be living with two other teachers (an American man of a similar age and an older English woman) I had no idea what to expect.

## 'WHY ARE YOU GOING THERE?'

We drove for around forty minutes before reaching a set of imposing tower blocks, one of which would be my new home. Whilst the taxi driver had little difficulty finding the actual street, finding the apartment building itself was slightly more difficult. The problem is that every building looks identical. Indeed, in the era prior to Yandex Maps (Russia's equivalent of Google Maps), I simply have no idea how people managed to find their way home through these concrete jungles. To my mind, there are only two possible explanations. Firstly, people simply did not leave home in the fear that they would not find their way back. Or, secondly, there was a vast wave of husbands who 'disappeared' after attempting to buy a loaf of bread at the local shop. In fact, the absurdity of Soviet architectural planning was even the subject of a classic 1976 Soviet comedy (*'The Irony of Fate, or Enjoy Your Bath'*). This film is immensely popular and is shown every year in Russia during the New Year celebrations.

In the film, the protagonist (Zhenya) gets drunk with his friends at a Moscow Banya (Russian sauna) before being put onto a flight to Leningrad (now St. Petersburg). Oblivious to the fact that he is no longer in Moscow, Zhenya provides his address to a local taxi driver. It transpires that there is an apartment of the same address in Leningrad which looks identical.

## 'WHY ARE YOU GOING THERE?'

Comically, Zhenya's key fits the lock of this identical apartment and he manages to pass out in a drunken stupor in a stranger's bed.

Whilst, this may seem exaggerated, it is in fact not that far from reality. For example, one thing I have already noticed during my short time in Russia is that every city has a 'Lenin Prospect' which is also usually home to a statue of the man himself. Similarly, there are many streets named after the famous Soviet cosmonaut Yuri Gagarin. Other streets are often named after Soviet heroes such as army generals or scientists. The Russian people have a strong sense of pride regarding their long and tumultuous history and this is reflected in their street names.

So, after circling the various apartment blocks for around five minutes, we eventually found the block which would be my new home. Upon entering the apartment I was greeted by my new housemates: Maria and Patrick. Maria was extremely welcoming and bubbly and Patrick greeted me with a well deserved beer. After going through the necessary formalities my manager left. That was it, I was home. Exhausted, after what had been a very long day, I soon passed out in bed. The unpacking could wait until tomorrow.

# 'WHY ARE YOU GOING THERE?'

## *Shopping*

The following afternoon, my new housemate Patrick took me to the local shopping centre which was home to a large supermarket called Auchan which would soon become my second home. I had no food and also needed some bedding and various items I hadn't been able to bring with me from England. The first hurdle I faced was managing to stay on my feet. Coming from the middle of England where there is little, if any, snow during winter, I was not prepared for the hazards of walking through snow and ice (despite having invested in some sturdy boots in England).

In fact, my first exit out of our apartment was far from graceful. As I followed Patrick out of our apartment building I managed to fall all the way down the steps leading down from our apartment. I landed in a crumpled heap at the bottom of the stairs on my stomach, legs and arms spread out wide as if I was swimming front crawl across the English Channel. Having heard my shriek, Patrick turned around and looked at me on the floor with a sense of bewilderment. However, realising my embarrassment, he was kind enough not to say anything or laugh, despite the obvious temptation. I picked myself up and carried on as if nothing had happened.

## 'WHY ARE YOU GOING THERE?'

After around twenty minutes, we reached the local shopping centre. Feeling a little peckish, we both headed to KFC. Here, is where I had my first (and certainly not last) bizarre communication in Russian. Having ordered my food on a self-service machine I then went up to the desk with my receipt to collect my order. Upon presenting my receipt the member of staff kept saying 'Dostavka' (Доставка) to me. I now know that this word means 'delivery' and he had somehow mistaken me for a food courier. However, at that time, I had no idea what this word meant. In a strange exchange, I proceeded to give the staff member my receipt with my order which he then ripped up and threw away. I then asked for this back. He obliged, handing me back my now torn receipt. Eventually, perplexed and hungry, I received my food.

Afterwards, we headed into the sprawling supermarket of Auchan where I bought all the necessary essentials for my first few days in Moscow. One thing which is interesting is that, due to EU sanctions, Russia has had to be creative in its sourcing of fruit and vegetables. I saw grapes from Moldova, peppers from India, as well as vegetables from countries as far flung as Iran. Nevertheless, I looked forward to trying my apples from North Korea.

## 'WHY ARE YOU GOING THERE?'

### *Training*

After a few days of settling into my new home, it was time to begin training for my new job as an English teacher. The training would last for one week, after which I would be placed into my very first school. In England, I had completed a TEFL (Teaching English as a Foreign Language) qualification which was a basic requirement for the job. This consisted of a weekend classroom course and a 100 hour online course.

In addition, in the six months leading up to my departure, I had been working for a reputable company based in China, teaching English to Chinese children online at the weekend. Due to the time difference, this often meant that I would be working at six o'clock on both Saturday and Sunday morning. As I was predominantly teaching children (some as young as five years old), I had to be energetic and somewhat loud which is not ideal when you live in a terraced house with neighbours either side. Despite my astounding lack of talent, I would often sing songs to keep the children entertained. One Saturday morning the neighbour pounded his fists on my front door as I was in the middle of 'If You're Happy and You Know It' with a student. At first, I thought he wanted to join in. However, given the force with which he was pounding on my door, I soon realised that, in fact, he was *not* happy and he wanted me to *know* it.

Thus, aside from the above, I did not have any real 'classroom' experience. Therefore, I was looking forward to my training which I hoped would stand me in good stead for the months ahead. As I made my way to the office (located a short walk away from the Kremlin) on my first day, I was also excited for another reason. This was the first time that I would be using the Moscow Metro. In typical Communist fashion, the Soviets designed something which resembles less a public transport system and more a work of art. There are chandeliers hanging from the ceiling, statues and artwork galore. It is truly beautiful. Indeed, my first experience of using this metro certainly proved to be memorable but not for the above reasons.

As I walked towards my local metro station in the west of Moscow, I was excited for the day ahead. Today was my first day of training. I would be meeting my new colleagues with whom I would be training as well as the various office staff. As already noted, the office was located a short walk away from the Kremlin so I was hopeful that I have chance to walk around Red Square as well, a place I had longed to visit for some time. One thing which is significantly different between the Moscow Metro and London Underground is the security situation.

## 'WHY ARE YOU GOING THERE?'

Here, in Moscow, security checks and bag inspections are routine. Personally, given the global threat of terrorism, I think this is an excellent idea and should be adopted in London.

However, as I strolled into my local metro station on this first day, I was completely unaware of these routine security checks and inspections. Just as I was about to tap my brand new Troika card (akin to London's Oyster card) on the machine, a small but terrifying lady wearing a uniform motioned towards me. I was then taken into a side room where I was told to place my bag into a machine for inspection.

As we waited to see whether I was carrying any explosives the lady began speaking to me in Russian. Despite answering to the best of my ability she could immediately tell from my accent that I was not Russian. At this point, a smile spread across her face. She obviously felt that my knowledge of weapons vocabulary in Russian was lacking as she then proceeded to teach me a variety of words for weapons. To enhance my understanding she made sure to demonstrate an action for each weapon. For example, she made a stabbing movement for a knife and so on. When we reached the word for 'gun' she formed a pistol with her hand which she rather unnervingly pointed in my direction.

## 'WHY ARE YOU GOING THERE?'

Eventually my bag check was complete and we parted ways. What was unclear, due to the smile on her face the entire time, was whether she was telling me that such weapons were prohibited or whether she was encouraging me to bring a weapon next time. I assumed the former but I could not be entirely sure. Having significantly strengthened my weapons vocabulary I bid her goodbye and continued my journey.

After a mere fifteen minutes on the metro, I reached my destination: Alexandrovsky Sad. This is a huge metro station in the heart of Moscow and is only a short walk away from the Kremlin. This station is also a transfer for various different lines on the metro which, at first, makes it a little confusing and overwhelming. I was told that I would be met here by my new manager. As I was walking through the station, I was struck not just by its beauty but also its size and depth. My journey down one of the escalators seemed to take so long that I looked at my watch to check what time it was.

With little else to do during this time, passengers simply stare at one another as if engaged in a staring contest. One thing which is noticeably different in Russia is that, unlike in England, people do not smile at strangers. In fact, if you do so, you are generally considered to have a mental impairment. Keen to keep a low profile on my first day out in

## 'WHY ARE YOU GOING THERE?'

Moscow, I decided to keep a straight face. A year older, I eventually reached the bottom of the escalators where I was met by my manager and fellow trainees (Lali and Liza) who have since become dear friends. After going up another set of escalators, we made the short walk to the office where we would be training.

Upon arrival, we were introduced to all the office staff who were incredibly friendly and welcoming. After grabbing a drink, we were then taken into one of the meeting rooms which would become our second home for the week. It was here that we were introduced to Frances who had drawn the short straw of training us. Frances was also a fellow Brit (as were the other trainees) and had a wicked sense of humour and relaxed attitude which immediately made me feel at ease. That was, until we discussed our work schedules for the following week.

"So, let's start with you Elliot, as your schedule is a little different", said Frances with a knowing grin on her face as she handed out our timetables. "Here, at this school on Thursday, you will be teaching Science", she announced. Great, I thought to myself. Given that I barely scraped a Grade C in GCSE Science at school, and could hardly operate a Bunsen burner without setting myself on fire, I felt significantly under qualified. Noticing the panic stricken look on my face, she was quick to reassure me that in fact the classes would be relatively easy. Apparently, teaching another subject in English was the latest trend in private schools in Moscow in an attempt to replicate the curriculum of international schools. Anyway, I was assured that all I would need to do each week was to create an 'experiment' (I was provided with a handout of lesson plans for the term) and let the children have fun, whilst hopefully learning a little English. There would be no need for Bunsen burners.

Feeling somewhat (although not entirely) relieved, Frances then went on to discuss one of the other private schools where I would be working which was based in a region outside of Moscow called Barvikha. I had not heard of this area before but, again, Frances had a knowing smile on her face which I found unsettling.

She explained that Barvikha was a very affluent area and that the children came from extremely wealthy families. She also went on to explain the various eccentricities of the school. There was a Spanish themed room with a mural on the wall as well as a 'British room', complete with rocking chairs. There were sofas in the classrooms and apparently (although I am still yet to see this) a picnic table in one room. Frances went on to explain that, rather than an ordinary school bell, in the morning, there was instead lively music which ranged from Latin American music to Gloria Gaynor's 'I Will Survive'. The children are usually taken to the school by their driver and I was told to expect to see seven year old girls dressed from head to toe in Gucci. It sounded amazing and bizarre at the same time. Nevertheless, I looked forward to teaching these rich kids how to speak in a Derbyshire accent. One thing was certain: I would not be bored at this new school.

# II.

# Work

## *Barvikha, 'The Bear Pit' and Science*

*A student's portrait of me lovingly created during class.*

## 'WHY ARE YOU GOING THERE?'

Since arriving in January I have primarily been teaching at three schools (two private schools and one State school), all of which have their own eccentricities. I will attempt to give a 'flavour' of these schools below. However, I am fully aware that some of the things I will describe are perhaps so strange that they have to be seen to be believed. Nevertheless, what I have learnt from working at these schools is that, given enough time, you can get used to anything. The extraordinary soon becomes the ordinary.

### *Barvikha*

One of the schools where I work, and in fact the school where I began my career as an English teacher, is a large private school in the affluent area of Barvikha. This is a 'luxury' village located around 25km away from the centre of Moscow. During the Soviet era, this village was home to the most desirable state dachas for government officials and leading intellectuals. In present times, it is home to the 'Barvikha Sanatorium', health resort of the Russian President. As you drive through the 'luxury village' (the school is actually based a few kilometres further west of the village) it certainly has the feel of a gated and exclusive community. There are row upon row of designer shops (Tom

## 'WHY ARE YOU GOING THERE?'

Ford, Gucci, Versace etc.) which my twelve year old students no doubt frequent for their weekend shopping trips. Everything is bold and loud and in your face. There is nothing subtle about Barvikha. This is home to the rich and the powerful and they want you to know it.

On my first day at this school it is safe to say that I was slightly nervous. This was my first time being thrown into a classroom as an English teacher. Frances escorted me to the school on this day and, upon arrival, we were greeted by the Head of the English department. After exchanging pleasantries, I was asked by the Head whether I spoke Russian to which I proudly responded 'Yes'. Her one word reply was short and to the point: 'Don't'. Russians are nothing if not direct. I actually find this quite refreshing, coming from a country where we rarely say what we mean. In Russia, people say exactly what they mean, nothing is left ambiguous. The Head explained that if the children found out that I spoke Russian they would try to speak to me in Russian rather than in English which would slightly defeat the purpose of my lessons.

After being shown around the school it was time to begin my first ever lesson as an English teacher. My first class was with Grade 1 (seven year olds). As if I wasn't nervous enough, I was told that both Frances and the Head would be observing this lesson. As the children stared at me, their eyes full of hope and excitement, I launched into a rousing rendition of 'The Hello Song'. We then did basic introductions before delving into the theme of the lesson which was 'family'. In spite of my lack of experience (and terrible singing) the class seemed to have gone well. Afterwards, pleased, or perhaps scarred, by what they had seen, Frances and the Head left me to my own devices for the rest of the school day. That was it; I was now a qualified English teacher.

Having worked at this school for several months, I can assure you, it is just as strange as I was promised. Firstly, let's start with the music. Every morning, at 08:55am, without fail, I will hear one of two songs (the school 'DJ' is kind enough to alternate the songs on a daily basis): Gloria Gaynor's 'I Will Survive' (in full) or a Latin American medley. Why use an ordinary school bell when you can play 1970s disco classics instead? My personal preference is 'I Will Survive' as I find that it lifts my spirits on a cold Monday morning. However, I am often sat in 'the Spanish room' at this time of day, thus the Latin American music seems much more fitting as I stare at the mural of Madrid on the wall. It is as if I am there. Almost.

## 'WHY ARE YOU GOING THERE?'

Another eccentricity of this school is its 'celebrations'. Now, generally, in Russia there are a lot of public holidays, certainly compared to England. However, despite this, there was one celebration which my school deemed to have been neglected by the Russian government: Orange Day. Now, on the off chance that you are not familiar with this holiday, let me elaborate. Orange Day usually takes place during winter, around March (I am unsure if it is fixed each year). The basic premise of Orange Day is simple: the weather in Russia at this time of year is dismal and so everyone should eat oranges to cheer themselves up. The Head of English seemed considerably apathetic as she explained this to me, suggesting that she is not a true believer of Orange Day. Nevertheless, I was just glad to have some sort of explanation as to why Dima had brought twenty mandarins into my classroom. Based on the look of elation on Dima's face, I would say that this year's Orange Day was a resounding success and I look forward to next year.

Another holiday which is widely celebrated is Maslenitsa. Unlike Orange Day (which is surprisingly restricted to my school and is not *yet* a national success), this holiday is celebrated throughout Russia as well as other Eastern Orthodox countries such as Ukraine and Belarus. This religious holiday takes place in the last week before

## 'WHY ARE YOU GOING THERE?'

Great Lent and denotes the beginning of Spring. However, I must admit that, as I was watching one of many Maslenitsa concerts in Moscow, surrounded by ten feet of snow, the celebration of Spring felt slightly premature. Not wanting to miss out on the action, my school made sure to celebrate this holiday. A huge Maslenitsa doll (similar to a scarecrow) was erected in the playground which the children proceeded to dance around one afternoon. No one had thought to tell me of these plans and so I found myself sat in a rocking chair in 'the British room', wondering where my private student was.

The final, and perhaps most important, comment I would like to make regarding this school relates to the students' behaviour. This can be captured in one word: dreadful. As already noted, the students come from extremely wealthy and privileged families and sadly this shows. More often than not, the children at this school view education as an inconvenient interruption to Instagram which makes teaching here particularly challenging. Whilst the younger children (Grades 1-4) are by and large a delight to teach, the same cannot be said of the older children I teach (Grade 5 and 6 in particular) who show a general disdain towards my lessons.

## 'WHY ARE YOU GOING THERE?'

For example, in 'the Spanish room' there are several sofas. In my view, whoever thought that placing sofas in a classroom was a good idea should be exiled to Siberia. At the beginning of one Grade 5 lesson, a student entered the classroom and immediately proceeded to lie down on one of the sofas. "Get up", I said, to which the student replied "No". We went through this exercise three times. On the final occasion, having lost my patience, I substituted the 'up' for 'out'. Happy to leave the classroom, the student obliged. On another occasion, the same student decided that the correct answer to every question on my worksheet was Kakashka (какашка) which roughly translates as 'turd'. Surprisingly, he did not receive any marks. On a separate occasion, I stood and watched another Grade 5 child unsuccessfully attempt (several times) to spell 'bitch' on the whiteboard, each time missing the rather key letter 'I'.

On the other hand, I should add that there are of course exceptions to the rule, and some children truly are a delight to teach. For example, one afternoon at this school I was waiting for students to attend my 'speaking club'. As far as I understand, this is a voluntary class for the students, thus explaining the fact that ironically I often spend this class sat by myself in silence. On this occasion, only one student turned up. Sasha is a Grade 5 student with impeccable manners and a maturity beyond his years. As the only student to attend, I advised him that it was probably not wise to do a debate in this lesson as planned. Instead, I simply asked him what he was passionate about and anything he would like to discuss. Now, usually, at this school the students can see no further than their social media pages and their career plans consist of vague notions of 'running a business' and earning lots of money. With this in mind, I was fairly taken aback by what happened next.

Rather than talk about money, businesses or other trivial things, Sasha proceeded to tell me all about his plans to open up a recycling factory in Moscow. I watched as he drew out his plans on the whiteboard in detail. He told me that he had had these plans from an early age and lamented the lack of any proper recycling facilities in the country, let alone Moscow. I should add that, despite minor improvements in recent years, there is no comprehensive recycling system or infrastructure in Russia. Additionally, there seems to be little public understanding or awareness of the issue.

Sasha's plans were extraordinary detailed and meticulous. I watched and listened in awe over the next forty minutes as Sasha explained his plans and how he would achieve them. It was nothing short of inspirational. As I listened, I couldn't help but worry that as he got older people might try to dissuade Sasha from his plans, instead encouraging him to chase money or other more trivial things. Particularly, given the wealthy environment by which he is surrounded. With this in mind, at the end of the lesson, I told Sasha that he *needed* to carry out this plan and not to let anyone tell him otherwise. I will not forget this lesson and I hope that Sasha does not either.

### *'The Bear Pit'*

Another school where I have been working for the past five months is affectionately known as 'The Bear Pit' due to the students' poor behaviour. This is a State school based in North West Moscow. Sadly, 'The Bear Pit' is not its official name but rather a nickname which has circulated through our company based on its reputation. In Russia, State schools are simply given a number and so its official name is much less exciting and is something along the lines of 'State School Number 14648465845'. I also usually refer to the school as 'soomashedshaya skola' (сумасшедшая школа) which translates as 'crazy school'. However, in the interests of avoiding confusion, I will use the most popular and accurate name of 'The Bear Pit' from here on.

## 'WHY ARE YOU GOING THERE?'

'The Bear Pit' was not included in my first week's schedule and so it was only in my second week that I began teaching here. At the time, I was assured that I would only be working at this school temporarily pending the imminent arrival of a new teacher. However, five months later, it did not feel very temporary and in fact I felt like I had been working there a lifetime. My first day at this school was a complete disaster. I was escorted to the school by Frances and, I can honestly say that, even by Russian standards, this school was incredibly disorganised. When we arrived, no one at the school could point us in the direction of my classroom or of anyone with any kind of authority. Eventually, we were 'greeted' (she didn't seem particularly pleased to see us) by a woman who seemed to be in charge and showed me to my classroom.

"OK, Elliot", said the woman, "So here is your classroom where you will be teaching Maths". Of course no one had informed me of this beforehand and so I was completely unprepared. I tried explaining this to the woman and asked that I be able to teach English (the irony of an English teacher asking to teach English was not lost on me) but she remained unmoved. I should add that, alongside Science, Maths was my least favourite subject at school and this had been reflected in my grades. Despite my pleading, I was ushered into the classroom and abandoned. As I entered the classroom I was greeted by around ten Grade 5 students who expected a Maths lesson. I had no idea what to do. After what seemed like several minutes of simply staring at the students I decided that this was not a long term solution and that I needed to do something.

"So, who can spell subtraction?" I asked, offering my whiteboard pen to the students. As they came up to the whiteboard one by one, each student struggled to spell the word correctly. The remainder of the lesson consisted of me asking them to spell various mathematical terms such as 'addition', 'fraction', 'division' and so on. Not one student could successfully spell any of these terms. "Great", I thought to myself, "this will keep them entertained over the next few weeks". I was hoping that their spelling would not improve in the interim as otherwise I was in trouble. As the clock approached seven, I decided that it was time to head home. I was weary but pleased that I had managed to survive my first day at 'The Bear Pit'.

Five months later, my Maths lessons have somewhat evolved since those early days. I now at least have a structure. The first part of the lesson usually consists of the students completing some exercises in a Maths textbook. This Maths textbook had been thrown at me one day by the aforementioned woman as she insisted that the students work from the book. When I asked her which section of the book the students were currently working on she had no idea and simply shrugged. For the second part of the lesson, I provide the students with handouts such as a Sudoku in an attempt to get them think critically. Sadly, this rarely succeeds. For example, in my most recent Grade 5 lesson we studied 'fractions'. However, rather than complete the worksheet which I had lovingly prepared, one of my students opted instead to draw a picture of a giraffe, elephant and Santa, all of whom were defecating. The link to fractions was tenuous at best.

Whilst my lessons may have evolved, sadly my students' behaviour has not. It is genuinely a shame that 'The Bear Pit' does not live up to its name and only enrol bears as students, as I'm sure that they would be better behaved. The examples of poor behaviour which I have witnessed during my time at this school would suffice to form a book in itself. Alas, in the interests of brevity I will instead pick a few highlights (or perhaps more accurately 'lowlights').

## 'WHY ARE YOU GOING THERE?'

For example, during one lesson early on in my tenure at this school, I turned away from the whiteboard to see two students choking one another. In fact, this description is not strictly accurate as it suggests the choking was mutual. In reality, it was one student choking another. I should add that the perpetrator was Russian whereas the victim was Georgian. This is worth noting as the two countries have not been on particularly friendly terms since the 2008 war, following which Russia occupied Abkhazia and South Ossetia. In more recent times, flights from Russia to Georgia have been banned by the Russian government. This decision followed widespread outrage and protests in the capital of Tbilisi after a Russian MP attempted to chair a session of the Georgian parliament **(1)**.

At first, I was pleased that the students were entertained but, as the victim was beginning to lose consciousness, I decided that I should probably intervene. The fact that they were fighting rather than listening to my wisdom was disappointing. However, what I found more disappointing was the look of concentration on the perpetrator's face as he was choking the other child versus the vacant stare that same student had given me earlier on in the lesson when I was teaching.

## 'WHY ARE YOU GOING THERE?'

On another occasion, one of my 'favourite' Grade 5 students decided that he would prefer to put a plastic bag on his head rather than attempt my worksheet. Unfortunately, it turned out that his head was slightly larger than average and so this was a somewhat difficult task. However, Russian children are nothing if not determined. Via the assistance of his friend he eventually managed to get the bag over his head. This took several minutes. However, the bag then ripped so he put it over his mouth instead and pretended it was a gas mask. I should add that I watched this whole series of events unfold with keen interest in the hope that the student may suffocate himself. Alas, this was not the case.

The previous week, this same student had taken a video of me on his tablet. As he did so he shook the tablet as if to create the impression that I was dancing. The was accompanied by a delightful Russian song titled 'Ya lubloo Minecraft' (я люблю Minecraft) which translates as 'I love Minecraft'. For those like me who are not well versed in computer games, Minecraft is apparently a game about 'placing blocks and going on adventures'. I couldn't be angry as it was actually quite funny. Nevertheless, I decided to take the tablet off him and lock him in a cupboard where he still remains. Of course that's a joke. I let him keep his tablet. I have no idea about the final destination of this video but I assume that somewhere, circulating on Russian social media, is a video of me 'dancing' to a song about a computer game.

Finally, a summary of this school would be incomplete without a brief mention of the musical situation. Now, in the part of the school where I teach Grade 5 and 6, there is no music at all. Music was probably deemed superfluous here due to the regular shouting and screaming of the students which deafens the ears instead. However, my first class of the day at this school is with Grade 1 and this classroom is located in a different part of the building. When I began at this school it was January and the 'school bell' was a rousing rendition of 'Jingle Bells'. I should add that in Russia, Christmas is in fact celebrated according to the Orthodox calendar and so takes place in January. Thus, 'Jingle Bells' in January in and of itself was not unusual. However, in May my Grade 1 class was interrupted three times by 'Jingle Bells'. This is unacceptable.

## 'WHY ARE YOU GOING THERE?'

### *Science*

Last but certainly not least, is a small and rather charming (aside from the gaudy yellow paintwork) private school based in West Moscow, at which I teach 'Science'. Of the three schools, I would actually say that this school is my favourite. This is primarily due to the fact that, in general, the students are well behaved. I teach at this school once a week and teach Grades 2 to 4. As I mentioned earlier, alongside Maths, Science was my least favourite subject at school.

As already noted, teaching other subjects in English is the latest trend in private Russian schools, in an attempt to mimic the curriculum of prestigious International Schools. I should add that, at International Schools they actually hire teachers who are qualified in that subject, rather than English teachers like me who reached the dizzy heights of Grade C in GCSE Science. Nevertheless, I had been reassured during my training week with Frances that all I would be required to do was to devise an 'experiment' and let the kids enjoy themselves whilst hopefully speaking a little English. After five months of teaching 'Science' at this school I can honestly say that it has been 'interesting'. The problem is not the students' behaviour which, by and large, has been fine. The problem lies in creating an experiment that actually works.

For example, in one lesson I tried to do an experiment called 'cloud in a bottle'. Sadly, whilst there was a bottle, there was no cloud. For this experiment you need: a water bottle with a sports cap, some hot water and a match. First, you pour some hot water into your water bottle. Then, you light a match and proceed to blow this out. As the match is smoking you squeeze the water bottle to suck in this smoke and then close the cap. Next, you gently squeeze the water bottle several times, after which a 'cloud' should form inside the bottle.

Please do not try this experiment at home. Not because it's dangerous but because it doesn't work. For five hours, I had my students lighting matches, blowing them out and then squeezing a water bottle. They were very confused, as was I. At the end of the lesson one student said to me "this was a very bad experiment". He said this twice which I thought was a little dramatic but it was hard to disagree. I should add that this lesson was observed by two of my office colleagues as part of my monthly observations.

## 'WHY ARE YOU GOING THERE?'

On another occasion, I *tried* a different experiment. Several weeks before, my colleague who worked in the classroom next door had done an experiment involving cornstarch. Apparently when you mix cornstarch with water it creates a mixture which acts as both a solid and a liquid. If you apply quick force such as a punch to the mixture it is solid. However, if you apply gentle force to it, it acts as a liquid. My students had been begging me to do this same experiment and eventually I relented. Needless to say, as with most of my experiments, it did not go well.

Firstly, when I arrived at the school on the morning of my class I realised that I had actually managed to buy gluten free cornstarch. I immediately understood that this was a problem as gluten is the ingredient which binds things together. I learnt this from my mother who is gluten intolerant and whose diet essentially consists of cardboard. So, during the break after my first class, I hurried to the local shop and proceeded to buy five packs of cornflour.

What I didn't realise was that there is a subtle distinction between cornflour and cornstarch. I needed the latter. My colleague is American and had used the word 'cornstarch' when discussing the experiment. However, naively, I thought that this was just the American term for cornflour. I was wrong. So, off I went again to the shop. My colleague kindly offered to look after my students in the meantime. As I rushed out the school I explained to the security guard that I was going to the shop, to which he replied 'apyat?' (опять), which means 'again'. "Yes", I muttered, stressed and tired.

Upon my return, I was met by a very official looking lady wearing a white coat. She was speaking to me very quickly in Russian and was evidently not happy. I did not understand everything but heard the word for 'dirty' and knew that there was a problem. Sure enough, as I headed back in the direction of my classroom it was carnage. There was flour everywhere. On the walls, floor and sofas (yes more sofas).

Whilst I had been very grateful for my colleague's offer, it is safe to say that I would not hire him as a babysitter. The whole area resembled the set of a horror movie directed by Delia Smith. The coordinator for the English language department had the misfortune of clearing up this mess. I of course offered to help but she just sighed and informed me that there were to be no more experiments today. With that, I sheepishly returned to my classroom. I took my five bags of cornstarch and placed them next to the five bags of cornflour in a cupboard where they still remain.

## 'WHY ARE YOU GOING THERE?'

A final experiment which I would like to mention involves vinegar, baking soda, a balloon and water bottle. For this experiment, you fill half a water bottle with vinegar. Then, you pour some baking soda into a balloon which you then stretch over the lid of the water bottle. Once ready, you pour the baking soda into the water bottle. The combination of vinegar and baking soda creates a pressure which inflates the balloon. Now, unlike my previous experiments, this one actually worked, albeit a little too well. The first student who tried this experiment was not holding the balloon correctly and so the mixture blew up in her face. Luckily she saw the funny side and only lost sight in one of her eyes so it could have been a lot worse. The remainder of the students equally enjoyed this experiment which I thought was a triumphant success.

However, after what I thought had been a successful lesson, white coat lady returned and simply said one word to me in Russian: 'akkuratna' (аккуратно) which means 'careful' and then walked off. I should have taken this as a warning. Sure enough, shortly afterwards the coordinator returned and told me that the whole school smelt of vinegar and that I was to stop this experiment immediately. So, yet again, my experiment was over before it even really began. I have heard through the grapevine that the school is not intending to continue with Science lessons in the following academic year. I cannot say that I am surprised. However, I do wonder what will happen to all that cornflour and cornstarch.

# 'WHY ARE YOU GOING THERE?'

# III.

# Leisure

## *Haircuts, Skating and Saunas*

*Taken minutes before falling over (again!) whilst cross-country skiing in my local park.*

## 'WHY ARE YOU GOING THERE?'

Now, as the popular proverb goes "all work and no play makes Jack a dull boy". So, having discussed my work at length in the previous chapter, it is now time to discuss how I have been spending my leisure time in the wonderful city that is Moscow. Before coming to Moscow I said to myself that I would try anything once (and twice if I liked it). In the short time in which I have been here, I have already tried cross country skiing, ice skating and horse riding. It is safe to say that I will not be representing the UK in the 2020 Olympics in any of these sports.

### *Cross-country skiing and Ice Skating*

A few days after arriving in Moscow, I felt that I had mastered how to walk in the snow without falling on my backside. Naturally, I decided it was time to try my hand at some winter sports. Of course, I had never done any winter sports in England because it requires an actual winter. Nevertheless, I decided that 'when in Moscow, do as the Muscovites do'. I started with cross-country skiing. Around a twenty minute walk from my apartment is a beautiful park. At the time (early January), the park was covered in snow and you could ski through it using the various tracks which had been created. Keen to show me one of her favourite winter pastimes, my housemate Maria offered to take me skiing and, for some unknown reason, I agreed.

After securing the skis to my feet (which was no minor feat), I was ready and off we went. I would love to describe here the beauty of a Moscow park in winter, however, this is impossible. It is impossible not because its beauty is beyond words (although some of the parks here truly are stunning), but because I spent the majority of my time on my back looking up at the sky, rather than appreciating the scenery. An hour later, I found myself crawling on my hands and knees back to the office from where we had hired our skis. I was panting, mouth wide open, like a Staffordshire bull terrier on a hot summer day. I vowed that I would never do this again.

Despite this, and against my better judgement, I did in fact go skiing again. On this second occasion, I was slightly better and spent considerably more time on my feet. Feeling more confident, I tried a more adventurous route through the park. This was a bad idea. Towards the end of the hour, I found myself hurtling towards a tree at an alarming speed. My legs were wide apart and I was in serious danger of losing my manhood. Luckily, I fell over before I reached the tree. This day marked the end of my cross-country skiing career.

# 'WHY ARE YOU GOING THERE?'

Undeterred by my experiences as a cross-country skier, I subsequently agreed to go ice skating with my new colleagues a few days later. The venue was Gorky Park. This is perhaps the most famous and, as far as I am aware, largest park in Moscow. In summer, there are people dancing, ice cream stalls and restaurants galore. However, during winter, the park is turned into an outdoor skating rink complete with lights and music. We went on a Sunday evening which was perhaps not advisable for a novice such as myself as this is one of the busiest times. After putting on my skates and waddling onto the rink like an overweight penguin, I was ready.

What I hadn't anticipated was how difficult it would be to actually stand up in skates. I have a new found admiration for Moscow's women who gracefully glide through the snow and ice in high heels during the winter. Lacking any natural ability, I found myself waddling around the rink for several hours, my right hand holding on to the wall and my left hand being held by my colleague.

On several occasions, feeling a little more confident, I let go of both wall and colleague but soon found myself doing what can only be described as the cancan before gripping onto the wall again in a mad panic. Meanwhile, seven year old Russian girls would whizz past me with annoying ease. Eventually, the inevitable happened, and I fell over.

## 'WHY ARE YOU GOING THERE?'

Alarmed, and perhaps fed up of feeling like she was teaching a toddler how to walk, my colleague took me to a rink side café where I remained for the rest of the evening, nursing my injuries with a Mulled Wine.

Now, I am aware of the expression 'a bad workman always blames his tools'. However, I honestly feel that there was a mechanical problem with my skates. For example, each time a family was taking a photograph I would end up hurtling towards them at great speed, managing to get myself in the photo at the last minute. I genuinely had no control over this. It was almost as if my skates had been fixed with some magnetic forces pulling me towards anyone with a camera. Some families appreciated the enthusiasm, others less so. Nevertheless, invited or uninvited, I managed to get myself in many family photos that night, which was perhaps the one and only highlight.

# 'WHY ARE YOU GOING THERE?'

## *Saunas and Haircuts*

Like any cosmopolitan city, Moscow has its fair share of stylish and well dressed people. Not wanting to stand out as the unfashionable British guy, I decided that I would need to take action if I was to blend in with the stylish Muscovites. I am not sure whether my attempts to do so have been successful but I have given it my best shot.

Firstly, I decided to join a gym. After doing some research I found out that the top floor of my local shopping centre was home to a popular, and most importantly, affordable, gym chain. The last gym I attended in England was located in a basement. In light of this, I didn't have particularly high expectations or requirements. If there was natural light and I didn't have to go underground, I would be happy. However, I still decided that it would be prudent to have a tour of the gym before I signed up. I was shown around the gym by one of the personal trainers who knew a little English. As with all of the Russian men in the gym, he was huge, covered in tattoos and had an impressive beard. He was terrifying. The tour was brief: "here are the weights and here is the cardio equipment", he said. That was it. He was certainly no tour guide but, pleased with what I had seen, I signed up for an eight month membership. I was relishing the prospect of working out in natural daylight.

At the time of joining the gym, I was informed that access to a sauna was included in my membership. My previous basement gym did not have such luxuries and so this was definitely a plus for me. For those who are not aware, saunas are very popular in Russia. Particularly popular and unique to Russia is the Banya. In short, a Banya is a traditional Russian bathhouse where you sit in a small room or building whilst you are hit with dried branches and leaves. Not quite ready to be beaten by a large Russian man with a tree, I thought that an ordinary sauna would be a good compromise. I could relax in the heat and steam without the fear of imminent pain.

However, what I hadn't been informed of was the rather unique dress code for a Russian sauna. Now, I am no prude but when attending saunas previously in the UK I, like everyone else, would wear a towel around my waist. In contrast, what I have learnt already in my few visits to the sauna here is that Russians view towels as a superfluous and cumbersome accessory the moment they enter the sauna. Upon arrival, men proudly remove their towel with everything on display. On one occasion, I walked into the sauna to find a man sat in a meditation position with his legs spread out wide, leaving little to the imagination. Most importantly, his eyes were wide open and he clearly wasn't meditating. The only conclusion I could draw from this was that he was simply doing this to annoy me. On another occasion, a man walked into the sauna wearing nothing but a felt hat.

Also central to my plan of becoming a stylish Muscovite was finding a good hairdresser. It is safe to say that I have never been particularly adventurous with my haircuts, especially in recent years. When I was at school I had a quiff which, as my mum kindly reminds me, I would spray gold for non uniform day. However, in recent years I have opted for a more traditional short back and sides. In fact, I had always gone to the same hairdressers in England. However, not fancying the commute back to England every four weeks for a haircut; I decided that I needed to find a new hairdresser.

After doing some research online, I managed to find a trendy chain of barbershops by the name of 'Top Gun'. It turned out that this chain had a barbershop located within walking distance of my apartment so I booked an appointment online and off I went. Now, although my usual haircut was not particularly difficult, I was still somewhat anxious in the knowledge that hairdressers sometimes have a tendency to get carried away. The added

# 'WHY ARE YOU GOING THERE?'

complication of course was that I would have to explain my preferences in a foreign language.

Upon arrival, I was greeted by two men, one of whom was called Isak and was from Kyrgyzstan. He would become my new barber. As soon as I walked into this barbers I felt out of place. There was music playing, flat screen televisions and fashion magazines. It was a far cry from my hairdressers back home which was run by two middle aged men and where the conversation largely consisted of complaining about the local football team's poor performance at the weekend. Nevertheless, perhaps it was time for a change, I thought to myself.

After being shown to a chair, it was time to explain what I wanted. Aside from a few words, Isak did not know any English. Luckily, there is an international grading system for men's haircuts and so we settled on grade 3 on top and grade 1 at the back and sides. Naively I thought that was that and I started to relax. All of a sudden, Isak then asked me whether I wanted a 'fade'. I had no idea what this was. Through a combination of hand movements and Russian he explained that a fade is the name for a technique where your hair on the back of your head gets shorter (and hence lighter, explaining the term 'fade') as it goes down. "Sure", I replied. The haircut itself took a total of forty minutes and was incredibly thorough. Back in the UK I would have had my haircut and done my weekly food shop within this same time. Overall, I was extremely pleased and have been a loyal customer ever since.

In the months which have followed I have managed to establish myself as a 'regular' at this barbershop where I am now affectionately known as 'Mister Elliot'. With my Russian improving, I feel able to have a good conversation with my hairdresser and feel extremely welcome there. However, as perhaps their only English customer, I remain somewhat of a novelty and have even become the face of the barbershop on Instagram. I never expected to turn into an Instagram celebrity when I arrived in Russia but having been thrust into the limelight there is nothing I can do. After each haircut, I am asked to complete a short video in English for their Instagram page. As with their haircuts, the barbershop expects top quality footage. I would be lying if I said that the pressure didn't sometimes get to me.

In the early days of my Instagram career the recordings were not exactly smooth which usually meant that I was required to perform the same video twenty seven times before I could leave the barbershop. What I am essentially saying is that I have been kept hostage by my hairdresser on multiple occasions. Now, however, I am a natural before the camera and the whole process usually takes no more than a few minutes. In my most recent video, I announced that I was leaving Moscow for summer but reassured my followers that I'll be back in September. I sounded like Arnold Schwarzenegger. I just hoped that my legion of followers would survive the summer without my monthly words of wisdom.

### *Horse Riding*

Last, but certainly not least, I have also tried my hand at horse riding since coming to Moscow. This was also a new experience for me and, as I lived to tell the tale, I can say that it was a success. However, like the winter sports I described earlier, my definition of 'success' is somewhat limited. If I do not kill myself or others in the process, then I consider the activity to have been a 'success'. I clarify this here for fear that you might otherwise consider me to have displayed some form of skill or natural ability in horse riding. Sadly, this was not the case.

This whole experience arose via my Russian teacher who, it turned out, had a friend who was a horse riding instructor. As ever, keen to try something new, a friend and I travelled with my Russian teacher to some stables in a small village outside of Moscow. Unlike me, my friend had previously ridden horses and so had some experience. Aware of my lack of horse riding experience (either divulged to her by my Russian teacher beforehand or just evident from the look of panic on my face), my instructor led me to my horse. He was old, tired and did not look in the mood to be sat on for two hours. After some brief safety instructions in Russian (half of which I did not understand), we were on our way. A helmet was apparently deemed superfluous.

The first part of the ride was distinctly underwhelming. As we exited the stables we rode through what, at first sight, looked like an industrial estate, with rubbish everywhere. It felt as if we were riding around the back of a supermarket. However, after crossing over a busy road, we rode through a field which, unsurprisingly for Russia, led to a stunningly beautiful church. As we reached the church the sun was setting. Luckily, I had plenty of time to take in this wonderful scenery because I was actually riding what turned out to be a large sloth.

Trailing far behind the others, the instructor decided that drastic action was required if I was to catch up and told me to shout the word "reese" (рысь) which means trot or gallop. However, at the time, I mistook this word for the similarly pronounced word of "рис" (reese) which actually means rice. So, for two hours, I led myself to believe that I was shouting the word 'rice' which, for some unknown reason, would make my horse go faster. I thought that the instructor was actually just getting me to read out her weekly shopping list. Two hours later, I proudly returned to the stables on my horse, remarkably unscathed.

# 'WHY ARE YOU GOING THERE?'

# IV.

## Nightlife

### *Techno and Models*

*Hotel Ukraina which is home to a top-floor bar with a panoramic view of Moscow.*

## 'WHY ARE YOU GOING THERE?'

Moscow is widely known as the city which never sleeps. In fact, a Russian electronic artist who goes by the terrifying name of 'DJ Smash' even recorded a song called "Moscow Never Sleeps" in 2007. This single was apparently a big hit, reaching number one on the Moscow Airplay Chart. In light of this, any account of life in Moscow would be incomplete without a description of its nightlife. Below, I will describe two nights out in Moscow, each of which display rather different perspectives of the Moscow clubbing scene.

### *Techno: Technically awful*

After coming to the conclusion that I was perhaps not cut out for winter sports, I decided to try and find another way to enjoy my leisure time. If you take a walk around any city centre in England on a Saturday night then you will soon realise that there is one activity which the British excel at and that is drinking copious amounts of alcohol before passing out, either at home or, more often, in a random bush or street. Sadly, our reputation for irresponsible drinking (and consequently poor behaviour) is known worldwide largely due to the morons who, usually on stag dos, having had one too many beers, see fit to urinate on famous statues throughout Europe.

## 'WHY ARE YOU GOING THERE?'

Like Brits, Russians are also known for their ability to drink vast amounts of alcohol. However, whilst living here, I have noticed that the drinking culture in Russia is in fact incredibly different to that in England. In England, the majority of drinkers are binge drinkers, drinking very little during the week but then proceeding to drink fifty pints on a Saturday night followed by a kebab. In contrast, in Russia there are generally two types of people. First, there are those who, dedicated or perhaps obsessed with, a clean and healthy lifestyle, do not drink any alcohol at all. Second, there are alcoholics. When I use the term 'alcoholic' I am not referring to our petty Saturday night binge drinkers. I am referring to the guys who think nothing of having a nice cold alcoholic beverage on the metro at six o'clock on a Monday morning. In my experience there seems to be very little in between.

So, being a young Brit, and therefore experienced in drinking alcohol and dancing awkwardly, I thought that maybe this was one activity in which I might excel in Moscow. Finding myself at a loose end one Friday night, I decided to attend one of the infamous office parties which take place every other week. These parties usually consist of heavy drinking and smoking (a room full of smoke is probably not the best environment for an asthmatic such as myself), followed by a foray to a nearby club. This Friday night was like any other. By the time I arrived, the office staff were already considerably drunk. I could either play catch up (attempting to match a Russian in their consumption of alcohol is rarely a good idea), or admit defeat and steadily pace myself and observe everyone get increasingly more drunk. I opted for the latter.

By around midnight, it was decided that it was time to leave the office for a nearby club. However, there was a divide. One group wanted to head to the usual club which specialises in overpriced drinks and 90s pop music. Another group, wanted to head to a rather grittier or edgier 'techno' club. After endless discussion, the techno group came out on top and off we went. What the leaders of the techno group hadn't thought to mention was that they didn't have a clue where this club was located. Now, drunkenly walking around a city centre in the early hours of the morning is perhaps fairly entertaining in England. It is not so in Moscow in January when the temperature is -15 degrees and there is a real risk of developing hypothermia.

After around an hour of walking we eventually found the club. Upon arrival, my ears were met by something which I had been assured was music but I was not convinced. Each song was annoyingly repetitive and had an infuriating thumping beat, resembling the sounds of a construction site. For me,

## 'WHY ARE YOU GOING THERE?'

'techno' seems a strange name for a form of music the creation of which, to my ears, requires no technical ability or skill whatsoever. In an attempt to 'get in the mood' I had a drink and awkwardly swayed my hips in time to the 'music'. It did not work, it was still awful.

Observing the large amount of people in the club who seemed to be enjoying themselves I thought that perhaps the problem was with me. I was right. Unlike the majority of people in the room, I had not taken any illegal substances. I am sure that a large number of drug addictions start with people simply trying to 'enjoy' techno music. After less than an hour, a group of us (all of whom were utterly miserable) headed to the usual club for some 90s pop classics. However, for me, the mood had already been lost and shortly afterwards I ordered a taxi home. As always, on the way home, I found myself explaining to the Central Asian taxi driver why I was not married and did not have eight children. If this was what Moscow's nightlife had to offer, I was not impressed.

# 'WHY ARE YOU GOING THERE?'

## *My night (and morning) with a Russian model*

Perhaps unsurprisingly, I had not had the fortune of bumping into many models when living in Derby. What a difference a few months can make. I am now about to tell you about my night (and morning) with a Russian model. This constituted my second foray into the Moscow club scene which, needless to say, was considerably better than my night of techno.

First, it is probably necessary to clarify how I, a five foot six inch man from Derby, came into contact with a Russian model. I would of course love to say that when I came to Moscow, Russian women were throwing themselves at me. My former colleague had assured me that when I moved to Moscow I would be considered an 'exotic fruit' by women purely due to the fact that I was English. Sadly, this had not proven to be the case. In fact, my communication with a Russian model had begun when I was still in England and attempting to improve my Russian. There is a very popular website where you can find online language exchange partners.

## 'WHY ARE YOU GOING THERE?'

The idea of a language exchange is that you find someone who is learning your native language and who is a native in your target language (in my case Russian). These exchanges, if equal time is devoted to each language, can prove very useful. Anyway, we had been communicating on and off via Skype for around a year. When I arrived in Moscow we got back in touch and, as fate would have it, she resided in the building directly behind my new apartment. We proceeded to meet up a few times and continue our language exchange in person.

On the night in question, I was enjoying a quiet drink in a small pub with a few friends after a long day at Barvikha. As is probably evident from my earlier description of the behaviour at this school, the consumption of alcohol post-work is usually required. Feeling rather tired, I looked forward to a quiet drink followed by an early night. In fact, I had even declined an earlier invitation to one of the infamous office parties. In actuality, this night turned out to be anything but quiet.

As I was finishing my first pint I received a message from my aforementioned model friend. She said that she wanted to show me a bar called 'Mercedes Bar' which is located at the top of what used to be 'Hotel Ukraina' (now Radisson Hotel). The bar was located in one of the 'Seven Sisters' buildings of Moscow. The 'Seven Sisters' are an infamous group of seven Stalinist skyscrapers in Moscow built between 1947 and 1953 **(2)**. She assured me that the bar offered panoramic views of Moscow. Feeling rather tired, I hesitated. Then, as I looked around the small pub crowded with middle aged men, I came to a realisation. A model was asking to take *me* out to a bar located in a skyscraper in Moscow. All of a sudden, there seemed very little to think about. I bid farewell to my friends and hopped in a taxi which she had insistently booked for me which whisked me away back to my apartment where we would meet and continue our night.

After quickly changing into the outfit which I would usually wear when hanging out with models in Derby, I jumped into the taxi outside my apartment in which my friend was waiting for me. Around ten minutes later we arrived at an enormous Stalinist skyscraper overlooking the Moscow River, the top floor of which was home to an exclusive bar. The inside of the building was just as stunning, with marble floors and pillars. I felt slightly out of place. Eventually, we reached the top floor whereupon we were told that we had to hand in our coats at the cloakroom downstairs. My friend promptly thrust her fur coat into my hands and off I trudged downstairs whilst she enjoyed a cocktail. Upon my return I ordered a drink which, although expensive, was not as overpriced as I had expected. For a brief few moments, as I was sat overlooking Moscow, I relaxed and took in the view.

However, this moment of relaxation was short lived. Like most young Russian women, my friend did not want to miss out on what was a perfect opportunity to update her Instagram profile. So, after a few sips of my wine, I was appointed head photographer in what seemed to be a never ending photo shoot. Now, as anyone who knows me will tell you, I am not a particularly gifted photographer. I often have a tendency to crop out heads or other important body parts. Nevertheless, my friend would not take no for an answer and so the photo shoot began. Predictably, it did not take long for her to become frustrated with my lack of photography skills. "What is that?" she asked, after my fifth unsuccessful attempt to take a photograph of her sprawled across a sofa.

She proceeded to lecture me on how to take photographs, offering me a variety of tips. I pretended to be paying close attention but on the inside I was crying and pleading for the photo shoot to be over. I was taken back to my sleazy photo shoot of my sofa back at my home in Derby. Eventually, with no evident improvement in my photography skills, I was fired and replaced by a young Russian woman. I sank into my seat utterly defeated and exhausted.

Around fifteen minutes later, pleased with the work of my successor, my friend drew a close to the photo shoot and finally started to relax. After several hours, I noticed that the bar was starting to empty and I checked my watch to find that it was already three o'clock in the morning. Naively, I thought that our night was coming to a close. As we admired the view from one of the windows my friend pointed to another skyscraper which was home to a hotel called 'Lotte Plaza'. She announced that this was our next destination. Despite it being well past my bedtime, I of course did not refuse.

A mere five minutes later, we had reached our destination. We headed upstairs to the bar which was again on the top floor and offered panoramic views of Moscow. After reaching the top floor, my friend told me to wait whilst she checked inside the bar. I had no idea what she was checking but I hoped it was to ensure that there was no techno music playing. A few minutes later she ran out of the room like a giggling schoolgirl informing me that some of her friends were in the bar. She said that she would briefly go and speak to them and then introduce me. Like Hyacinth Bucket in the popular British sitcom 'Keeping up Appearances', my friend's social standing was clearly very important to her and so she couldn't reveal that she was friends with a young man from Derby. Instead, she insisted that she would introduce me as her new English teacher from London. Why not just introduce me as George Clooney I thought?

After around ten minutes of waiting alone in the lobby I became suspicious that my friend was playing a cruel trick on me. Perhaps I was about to be dragged into a different room by two burly Russian men, tied to a chair and subjected to techno music for several hours. If that was my fate then so be it, but I was tired of waiting in a lobby by myself so I text her and she told me to come in. I was introduced to two men, both of whom I estimated were in their late thirties and were evidently wealthy. The table was full of various expensive spirits. I was encouraged to help myself to some whisky. One of these men proceeded to repeatedly apologise to me for the next few hours saying that he could not speak English because he was drunk. Ironically, he said this in perfect English. In Russian, I managed to ascertain that he was a banker. The other man was much less friendly and was a man of few words. I thought it best not to ask what he did for work.

## 'WHY ARE YOU GOING THERE?'

Feeling rather settled and slightly intoxicated, I spent a few moments taking in my new surroundings. Seemingly unchanged from the late Soviet period, the bar was illuminated by delightful soft pink neon lighting. Luckily, there was no techno music this evening. Instead, my ears were met by Russian power ballads. Middle aged men would enthusiastically sing along to the songs, the lyrics of which were displayed on television screens across the room. The lyrics on the screen were accompanied by traditional backdrops such as the Kremlin and Putin riding a horse bare-chested across Siberia. It seems that such ballads can move grown men to tears, although I suspect that I was crying for different reasons to everyone else in the room.

At around six o'clock in the morning the bar began to empty out apart from fifty year old Dima who, fuelled by vodka, was continuing to enthusiastically boom out power ballads. I prepared myself for the journey home until I was reminded of DJ Smash's number one hit 'Moscow never sleeps'. We were going to another club my friend announced. This too had Russian karaoke she announced. Great, I thought to myself, as if this was some kind of incentive. I was shattered; perhaps the model lifestyle was not for me after all.

## 'WHY ARE YOU GOING THERE?'

I cannot remember much about this particular club as I was increasingly drunk and have since tried to wipe out any existing memory of Russian power ballads from my mind. I next remember departing from this club around eight o'clock in the morning and going to a nearby café for breakfast with some new Russian acquaintances. One of these acquaintances kept insisting that I have some of his sausages and eggs, saying that in Russian tradition it is customary for guests to eat first. I had never heard of this tradition and came to the conclusion that he had either poisoned the breakfast or it was terrible. Either way, I was not persuaded to try his sausages.

Around two hours later, my friend and I finally headed home in a taxi. It was around ten o'clock at this point. However, rather than allow me to crawl into bed my friend insisted that we go to a local pizzeria. At least I was within crawling distance of my apartment, the end was in sight. As I sat down, guzzling down a cappuccino and slice of pepperoni pizza, I suddenly realised that I was not wearing my glasses. In our drunken state this was obviously hilarious. A few hours later when I was sober and could not see where I was going it would not be as funny. Anyway, given that I had thought it a good idea to order pizza for breakfast I decided that I was probably lacking capacity to find my glasses at this stage and resolved to deal with it later. At around eleven o'clock I finally returned to my apartment with neither my glasses nor dignity.

After several hours of sleep, I woke up later that afternoon and decided to walk around my local area in an attempt to find my glasses. Understandably, trying to find glasses when you wear glasses is rather difficult and I soon gave up hope. What I was successful in finding during the expedition of my local area was an extreme amount of dog excrement. I presume that few dog owners here choose to clear up their dogs' mess. Either that or there is one local dog with some incredibly bad bowels. Resigned to buying a new pair of glasses, I contacted my friend who kindly offered to guide me in my blind state to a nearby shopping centre. In fact, my friend was pleased to hear that I was still alive. At around three o'clock in the morning I had apparently sent her a drunken text simply saying "I do not know what is happening". When you get such a text from someone in Moscow at that time it is probably wise to assume the worst. Around £200 later I had a new pair of glasses and my sight back. Exhausted, I bid farewell to my colleague and headed home for a quiet Saturday night.

# V.

# The Moscow Metro

*Lenin, chandeliers and gold*

*Moscow's stunning Kievskaya metro station.*

## 'WHY ARE YOU GOING THERE?'

Apart from Red Square and the Kremlin, perhaps the most iconic feature of Moscow known worldwide is its monolithic and awe-inspiringly beautiful metro system. Indeed, there are very few public transport systems globally which are similarly decorated with glistening chandeliers and marble floors. As someone who now spends a vast part of his life underground, somewhat akin to a mole, I feel that I am well qualified to provide a few comments on one of the world's finest public transport systems. After a brief history of the Moscow Metro system, it is these observations to which I will then turn.

### *A brief history of the Moscow Metro*

The Moscow Metro first opened its doors to the public on 15 May 1935 at seven o'clock in the morning **(3)**. The first train consisted of two red carriages and the first journey commenced from the station of Сокольники (Sokolniki) and continued until Смоленская (Smolenskaya). Excitement and expectations were high, and rightly so, given Stalin's order that the metro stations be designed as 'palaces of the people'. The first line was a total of 11.2km long and consisted of thirteen stations. By the end of that year, intervals between trains had been reduced to just four minutes.

## 'WHY ARE YOU GOING THERE?'

Construction continued throughout the pre-war period, with a further six stations being built in 1938, including the beautifully ornate station of Маяковская (Mayakovskaya) which is named after the famous Soviet poet and playwright Vladimir Vladimirovich Mayakovsky. However, with the outbreak of World War Two, construction slowed down and many metro stations instead found themselves being used as air raid shelters. According to statistics, between the months of June and December 1941, a total of two hundred and thirteen children were born inside the Moscow Metro **(3)**. Following World War Two, expansion continued with the construction of the metro stations of Краснопресненская (Krasnopresnenskaya) and Киевская (Kievskaya) in 1954. In total, there were four initial stages of construction: the first stage (1935-1937, included the construction of Sokolniki station), the second stage (1937-1938, included the construction of Mayakovskaya station), the third stage (1938-1944) and the fourth stage (early to mid-1950s, included the construction of Kievskaya) **(4)**.

However, it should be emphasised that construction did not stop there and, in fact, continues right up until the present day. At the time of writing, work on an additional line known as the 'first diameter' is almost complete and is due to open towards the end of December 2019/ January 2020.

## 'WHY ARE YOU GOING THERE?'

Having briefly considered the history of the Moscow Metro, it is now time to discuss some of my experiences using the metro in modern-day Moscow.

### #1: A whole new world: The etiquette of the Moscow Metro

Firstly, for those considering taking a journey upon the Moscow Metro, please take note that, in doing so, you are not merely embarking upon a journey of public transport but rather a whole new underground world, for which exists a series of separate rules and etiquette: ignore these at your peril.

Indeed, perhaps the primary rule applies to young men and men in general. Should an elderly woman (or indeed gentleman) get on the train and find no seat, you should offer yours immediately. Even if they refuse to sit down (despite being in their eighties, sweating profusely and carrying 72 shopping bags), a failure to even offer your seat is considered a huge social *faux pas* and will result in angry stares in your direction for the remainder of your journey. I have often found a seat on the metro to my great delight only to stand up a moment later when a panting elderly woman hurtles in my direction.

## 'WHY ARE YOU GOING THERE?'

Now, even if you are lucky enough to find, and *keep*, your seat, I would advise you not to get too relaxed as the way in which you are sitting is most likely being analysed by your fellow passengers. For example, on one occasion, I was on the way home and was slightly worse for wear, having consumed a little alcohol. A little tired, I decided to rest my feet on the chair opposite me. This swiftly resulted in the anger of a fellow passenger who reprimanded me immediately, telling me that such behaviour was 'unpleasant'. In retrospect, I agree with him but the anger which it provoked in him seemed slightly extreme.

In addition, my friend Lali told me that she is often accosted for crossing her legs whilst sat on the metro. On one occasion a male passenger apparently even took it upon himself to pry her legs apart. I am not quite sure why it is unacceptable for women to cross their legs but fine, it seems, for men on the metro to sit with their legs as wide apart as possible as if stretching before about to partake in some gymnastics.

Finally, one thing I have observed in my time on the metro is that Russians seem to have somewhat of a phobia of missing their station. As such, if standing in the vicinity of the doors of the train (as is usually the case when crowded), you are likely to be tapped on the shoulder a total of ten times and asked a one word question: "Выходите?" This means, "Are you exiting the train at the next station?". From personal experience, I can assure you that after the fifth tap on the shoulder, you will most likely leave at the next station even if it is a two hour walk from where you are heading, just so you can stop being asked this question.

### #2: Bring your own: Things which people carry on the Metro

As is perhaps the case with any public transport system, you are often liable to see people transporting many weird and wonderful things. The Moscow Metro is no exception. For example, one of the most common things to see being transported on the metro (ironic given Russians' opposition to eating in public) is food. Often, understandably not wanting to brave the harsh weather conditions, many of the food delivery couriers instead opt to head underground. What this means is that, at precisely 12pm, when you are hungry and have not eaten for several hours, you are likely to have the waft of pizza underneath your nostrils, just to remind you of how hungry you actually are.

## 'WHY ARE YOU GOING THERE?'

In addition to this, other items which I have seen people transporting on the metro include balloons, flowers and animals. However, these are nothing compared to what I experienced a few weeks ago. On this particular day, I was travelling from Боровицкая (Borovitskaya) to my student's house who lives near Нагатинская (Nagatinskaya) metro. At this point, I should add that these stations are located on the grey line which is often fairly busy and perhaps explains the behaviour which I am about to describe.

As I got on the train at Боровицкая, I naively looked left and right to see whether there were any free seats for my twenty minute journey, regrettably there were not. It was when I looked to my right that I then saw an elderly gentleman sat, legs crossed, reading a newspaper on a wooden chair which he had evidently brought from home. However, I seemed to be the only one who found this strange. I asked the gentleman if I could do anything to make him feel more at home such as make him a coffee or bring him some slippers but he declined, saying that he didn't want to impose. A few stations later, the same gentleman stood up, picked up his chair and got off the train carrying his chair to its next destination. Although I mock, this man arguably had a right to feel smug, given that the rest of us were stood up crushed under each other's armpits.

# 'WHY ARE YOU GOING THERE?'

## #3: *The Invisible: Moscow's homeless community*

The sad reality is that in the majority of large cities around the world you will find a sizeable homeless community. Indeed, homelessness is a global problem and, more often than not, the causes and features of this social crisis are the same worldwide. However, living in Moscow, I have noticed subtle differences between homelessness in Russia and the UK. The main thing which has struck me deeply is the age of those who find themselves begging here in Russia.

By and large, in the UK, those begging on the street are usually fairly young and it is certainly very rare to see an elderly man or woman begging on the street. Whilst I am not an expert in this field, I assume that the reason for this is that in the UK there is a certain infrastructure and social safety net which prevents this from happening. However, distressingly, in Moscow it is commonplace to see elderly men and women begging on the street and inside the metro, holding signs asking for money for food and medicine.

As someone not accustomed to seeing this, I am finding it increasingly difficult to turn a blind eye to this crisis. Whilst I have not read much into this area, I have heard much of the inadequacies of State pensions in Russia. Of course, homelessness in any form, is regrettable but it feels particularly egregious to see eighty year old women begging for money. With harsh winter conditions, many of Moscow's homeless come into the metro in order to survive. Indeed, it is reported that eleven homeless people died during the winter of 2017-2018 **(5)**. Whilst this is much better than the year of 2003 where a total of 1,200 homeless people died from the cold, it is still unacceptable and a source of shame **(5)**. I hope that the Russian government is putting as much energy and resources into tackling this crisis as they are into expanding Moscow's wonderful metro system.

### #4: 'Palaces of the People'

As already noted, prior to their construction, Stalin ordered that Russia's metro stations be designed as 'palaces of the people'. As someone who travels on the Moscow Metro on a daily basis, I can confirm that its stations deserve this title. Whilst the beauty of Moscow's Metro system is already known worldwide, this cannot be emphasised too much and any discussion of the metro system would be remiss without a comment on its overwhelming splendour. For Muscovites born and raised here, they struggle to understand what all the fuss is about. Tell a Muscovite about your favourite metro station and they will look at you as if you are clinically insane.

## 'WHY ARE YOU GOING THERE?'

However, ask any foreigner in the city this same question and they will gladly give you a comprehensive answer.

For me, given that many of the stations are extraordinarily beautiful, I find it difficult to choose just one. However, there are several stations which stand out. For example, one such station is that of Новослободская (Novoslabodskaya). This station is on the brown line in the north of the city and was built in the early 1950s **(3)**. As you leave the train and head to the centre of the platform you are faced with dozens of beautifully crafted stained glass windows. As you gaze at these works of art, it is hard to remind yourself that you are inside a metro station and not in fact an ancient church.

Another equally beautiful station which I often use, due to its proximity to my apartment, is that of Киевская (Kievskaya). As already noted, this station was completed in 1954 and was therefore built in the fourth stage of initial construction. As its name suggests, this station has a Ukrainian theme and the walls are adorned with beautiful paintings set in Russia's neighbour. At the end of the central platform is a portrait of Vladimir Lenin which seems to be a favourite with eager Chinese tourists. In addition, you will find chandeliers hanging from the ceilings throughout the station as well as a lot of elaborate gold-trim embellishing its marble pylons.

## 'WHY ARE YOU GOING THERE?'

Unfortunately, as this station is a transfer station to several different lines, it is often extremely busy. This means that it is unwise to take too much time admiring its beauty, unless of course you fancy being hurled to the floor by an angry fellow passenger in a rush.

Another station worthy of mention is Площадь Революции (Ploshad Revolyutsii, meaning Revolution Square). This station is located in the centre of Moscow on the dark blue line and was built in 1938. This station contains a total of 76 bronze statues including, but not limited to, a male worker and enlisted soldier, miner, engineer and a male soldier with a dog **(6)**. Amongst the superstitious, many of these statues are thought to bring good luck, especially the dog accompanying the soldier. As such, passengers often rub this dog's nose for good luck. This is evident from the fact that this dog's nose is a highly polished gold due to regular wear.

Last, but certainly not least, is the aforementioned station of Маяковская (Mayakovskaya) which is named after the famous Soviet poet and playwright of the same name. This station is located on the green line in the centre of the city and is truly beautiful. It is most well known for its 34 ceiling mosaics depicting "24 Hours in the Land of the Soviets" **(7)**. Regrettably, this is not a station which I have had the good fortune to visit on many occasions but is certainly a station where you could spend hours getting lost in its beauty.

As can be seen from the above, the Moscow Metro is a weird and wonderful underground world separate to its over ground counterpart, and well deserving of its own chapter in this book. Having never travelled on the New York or Tokyo subway, or the Paris Metro, perhaps I am unqualified to say this, but I am of the firm view that the Moscow Metro is the most beautiful and best underground transport system in the world.

# VI.

# Rostov Veliky

*"Sorry, we have no more beer."*

*The monastery where we stayed in Rostov Veliky.*

# 'WHY ARE YOU GOING THERE?'

## *International Women's Day*

As I have already mentioned, there are a lot of public holidays in Russia, certainly compared to England. One such holiday is International Women's Day which takes place annually on the 8th of March. This is a day celebrating the social, economic, cultural and political achievements of women. As its name suggests, this celebration is not specific to Russia but is in fact a global celebration. However, this celebration is certainly given much more attention in Russia compared to England. Whereas in England it is a normal working day, in Russia it is an official public holiday.

On 8th March, every woman in Moscow, it seemed, had been given a bouquet of flowers in celebration. On this note, I should add that, almost every street in Russia is home to a florist. Flowers have an important place in Russian culture and are given for a variety of celebrations including, but not limited to: birthdays, dates and Teacher's Day. A word of warning: if you buy flowers in Russia, make sure to buy them in odd numbers. An even number of flowers are only given at funerals and would undoubtedly spell the death of any blossoming romantic relationship. The importance placed on flowers is one of many things I like about Russian culture.

## 'WHY ARE YOU GOING THERE?'

So, in the build up to International Women's Day, I was excited. Not because I had a string of women to whom I could provide flowers but because this celebration resulted in a three day weekend. This was a perfect opportunity for me to travel outside of Moscow, I thought. Discussing this with my British colleague Frances in the office one day, she suggested that I visit a town called Rostov Veliky. This was located several hours away from Moscow by train and forms part of the so-called 'Golden Ring'. The 'Golden Ring' is a group of ancient towns and cities in Russia located in a ring like arrangement. There are eight main cities/towns included in this group: Yaroslavl, Kostroma, Ivanovo, Suzdal, Vladimir, Sergiev Posad, Pereslavl-Zalessky and Rostov Veliky. Eager to see something new, I persuaded my friend Lali to join me. This would be a truly Russian experience as we would be staying in a monastery.

# 'WHY ARE YOU GOING THERE?'

## *Russian trains: tea, cakes and feet*

As well as being my first trip outside of Moscow, this weekend getaway was also the first time that I would be using the trains in Russia. I was of course excited to experience Russian trains but also slightly anxious. Given the vast size of Russia, missing your station could have drastic consequences. In England, the worst that could happen is that you end up stranded in Cornwall or Scotland. In Russia, you could easily end up in Siberia. I was not ready for a Siberian winter just yet.

When booking the train tickets online I opted for the cheaper seats in the belief that this would offer a more 'authentic' experience. I was not wrong. What I didn't realise was that, in addition to views of the vast wintery Russian countryside, I would also be provided with a view of a middle aged Russian man's feet for several hours. This was included in the price it seems. This man, who was opposite us, slept face down with his bare feet in my friend's face for the entire journey. In spite of this, my first Russian train journey was every bit as charming as I had hoped. My friend and I found ourselves sat at a little table with a net curtain and a small window. Another charming aspect of Russian trains is tea. Like flowers, tea also has an important place in Russian culture. When you order tea on a Russian train it comes in a delightful traditional glass in a silver holder. Several hours later, we arrived in Rostov, after what had been (feet aside) a perfectly pleasant train journey.

At this point, I should add that, the train on return to Moscow was an entirely different affair. On the way back we had opted for an express train and found ourselves travelling in comparative 'luxury'. The train had Wi-Fi and all other expected mod-cons. There was not a bare foot in sight. Thankfully, however, the serving of tea remained traditional.

Feeling a little peckish, my friend decided to buy a cake which had caught her eye on the trolley as the train assistant walked past. Unfortunately, this did not quite go to plan. As my friend handed over a relatively large note in payment, the assistant pocketed this but said that she didn't have any change at the moment but would provide her with this later. It was only once this woman had walked off that we realised there had been no exchange of a delicious chocolate product.

As the woman walked past several minutes later I urged my friend to correct this sorry state of affairs. She resisted, perhaps due to tiredness or on the misguided assumption that all would be resolved. Twenty minutes there was still no cake but the woman did bring her some change. My friend politely thanked this woman for her change for the cake which she bought but never received and that was that. I understood my friend's pain and confusion as I was reminded of my similarly bizarre transaction in KFC during my first weekend in Moscow.

### *Rostov Veliky: 'Sorry, we have no more beer'*

So, having discussed our journey to and from Rostov, it is now time to discuss the town itself which, quite honestly is beautiful. Rostov Veliky (not to be confused with the southern city of Rostov on Don) is a small town with an estimated population of around 30,000 people. At the heart of the town is its very own Kremlin. There is a Cathedral (Assumption Cathedral) and four Kremlin churches. Nearby there is also a large lake known as Lake Nero which was completely frozen over at the time of our trip and offers spectacular views of the Monastery of St. Jacob Saviour. All of these monasteries and churches are as stunning on the inside as out, decorated with gold, chandeliers and artwork. Sadly, I did also witness signs of neglect during my time in Rostov. Pavements and roads were in need of repair and beautiful buildings stood empty. Being such a tourist destination, it is a shame that more money is not invested into the area. I hope that this changes in the future.

## 'WHY ARE YOU GOING THERE?'

If, however, Rostov is to attract an increasing number of tourists, businesses should be prepared to extend their opening hours, at least past half past eight on a Friday night. If Moscow is the city which never sleeps, Rostov is the town which always sleeps. For example, on the Friday evening following our arrival we headed to a restaurant in the centre for some traditional Russian fare. Frances had assured me that once you leave Moscow (and St Petersburg) it is literally impossible to spend money. The difference in prices is due to the fact that everything in Russia is centered around Moscow and, to a lesser extent, St Petersburg. So, I was ready for some hearty Russian food at low prices.

I was not disappointed. The food was incredible and affordable. For two of us, having ordered several courses and a drink each, the total was around £10. There was a range of traditional food on offer, including, but not limited to, pelmeni (dumplings filled with meat/ cheese), borscht (beetroot soup) and a range of meats. Sadly, the same cannot be said for the service. The young waitress seemed slightly nervous, or at least I am assuming that is the reason she threw my cutlery in the direction of my face.

## 'WHY ARE YOU GOING THERE?'

The real problem began however when I tried to order a second beer. Having finished one beer I decided that I would indulge in a second. It was a Friday night after all. The waitress had forgotten about my request for another beer so I politely reminded her. With that, she went back to the kitchen and seemed engaged in lively conversation with whom I presume was the owner, for several minutes. Upon her return, she politely informed me that she was unable to provide me with a second beer as there was no more beer left in the entire restaurant.

Not taking the hint, my colleague and I then asked to see a dessert menu instead. With this, the same waitress picked up a nearby axe which I had wrongly assumed was only for decorative purposes and swung it in our direction. There would be no dessert or beer. It was closing time. It was half past eight on a Friday night. At the same time, all of the customers prepared to leave in a mass exodus which I had mistaken for a fire alarm. The locals were clearly better informed than ourselves. You do not order beer in Rostov after half past eight on a Friday night. If anyone tells you otherwise they are crazy. As the lights were being turned off, we finally took the hint that perhaps it was time to leave.

## 'WHY ARE YOU GOING THERE?'

After leaving the restaurant, somewhat bewildered, and with everything in the town closed, we decided it was time to head home. The monastery where we were staying (yes you read that correctly) was located around an hour walk away from the centre so we decided to book a taxi. Using a number for a local taxi firm which we had been given earlier in the day in a café, my friend called to book a taxi. After several minutes of waiting a lady answered who abruptly informed us that there were no more taxis available tonight and proceeded to hang up. With little other choice, we made our way back on foot to the monastery in our very own pilgrimage. The journey took over an hour and culminated in me falling on my backside outside a cemetery which was all the more ominous given the lack of any street lighting. Eventually, we reached the monastery which was closed. Luckily, we were let inside by an official looking security guard. We were exhausted and it was only ten o'clock.

As mentioned above, rather than staying in a hotel for our trip to Rostov, we opted to stay in a monastery for a truly authentic experience. This sounded like a great idea until we realised that our particular monastery was located an hour's walk away from the town centre. When booking the room online via a popular booking website, the only room available was a family room, consisting of six beds.

## 'WHY ARE YOU GOING THERE?'

This was barely more expensive than a double room anyway at the total price of £50 for the weekend. When we arrived at the monastery, our choice of a family room raised some eyebrows. The receptionist could not understand why, who she had presumed were a young couple without children, had opted for a family room. It turned out that other rooms were available at a cheaper price after all. Not wishing to get into the intricacies of why we did not want to share a double bed, we insisted on the family room to the receptionist's confusion. As an explanation for our choice of room we merely said that we liked our space.

Overall, and in all seriousness, Rostov Veliky is a wonderful and charming small town which is well worth a visit. However, if you are seeking a weekend of alcohol fuelled debauchery I suggest that you try Moscow or St Petersburg instead.

# VII.

# Dating

## *Taxis and Walking*

*Taxis heading down the busy street of Novy Arbat*

# 'WHY ARE YOU GOING THERE?'

## *Taxis*

After telling people in England that I was moving to Russia they would usually make two comments. The first comment would usually consist of some misguided joke about my impending death. The novelty of this began to wear off after a while. The second comment was that Russian women are beautiful. Having lived in Russia for a year, I can now confirm this. At first, I put this down to living in a large cosmopolitan capital city. Generally, wealthier, younger and more attractive people tend to congregate in capital cities such as Moscow, London etc. Capital cities are also home to a more diverse population.

However, this theory of mine fell flat after travelling outside of Moscow and noticing very little change in the proportion of attractive women. I can only assume that there is something in the water here. However, even if this is true, I would strongly advise against drinking the tap water here in the hope that it might make you more attractive. In fact, all you are likely to achieve is a serious bout of diarrhoea.

## 'WHY ARE YOU GOING THERE?'

For a variety of reasons, when in England, I had had little time for dating, and so, I decided it would be a good idea to dip my toes back into the world of dating. So, when in Moscow, I downloaded two popular online dating apps and waited for my inbox to be flooded with messages from Russian women wanting to try this 'exotic fruit' as my former colleague would say. This did not quite happen. Still, I am pleased to say that during my time here I have had several dates, the majority of which have resulted in perfectly pleasant and enjoyable evenings. However, of course, there have been some dates which have proven to be more interesting than others. Not wanting to bore you with an entire chronology of my dating history in Moscow, I will limit my discussion to these 'interesting' dates. It is these dates to which I now turn.

It was February 2019, and several weeks after downloading the aforementioned dating apps, my inbox had not filled up as expected. Perhaps I was not so exotic after all. I realised that if I was going to have any success in the ruthless world of online dating then I would need to be proactive. Having sent various messages (in Russian), I eventually found myself matched with a woman who, for the sake of anonymity, I will call Svetlana. She was a young woman of a similar age. I was aware that there was a strong possibility that we had matched only after she had inadvertently swiped the wrong way on my profile during some sort of seizure. However, perhaps she had intentionally liked my profile and so it was worth a shot, I thought. After exchanging various messages via this app (again in Russian as she did not speak English), we swapped phone numbers and soon agreed to meet up.

Prior to meeting up, I had been in charge of determining the arrangements. In my limited experience, it seems that Russian women generally prefer men to take the initiative. I had suggested meeting at a metro station in a fairly central location, from which we could then head to a restaurant. "No, you moron, I want to wear a dress. I will freeze to death", she replied. I was slightly taken aback. I will admit that the word moron (in Russian 'дебил', pronounced debeel) was not actually used, but it was implied. I considered telling her that, of all the places in wintery Moscow, the underground was probably the warmest and so she was unlikely to freeze to death. However, not wanting to ruin my chances at this early stage, I instead agreed to book her a taxi from her house. It turned out that she lived in the east of Moscow, literally on the other side of the city. Despite being an hour away, taxis in Moscow are cheap and cost within the region of £5.00 for such a journey.

## 'WHY ARE YOU GOING THERE?'

Having agreed on the mode of transport, it was time to agree on a venue. We decided to go to a restaurant but, again, the choice of restaurant was my responsibility. So, after scouring Google, I managed to narrow my search down to two restaurants and Svetlana chose one. So, having agreed upon a venue and mode of transport, all that was left was to try and make myself look presentable. This is by no means easy. By the end of the working week I usually looked fairly disheveled after teaching unruly children. The morning of the date I had a haircut and bought some flowers and, with that, I was ready.

That evening, I hopped on the metro (I was not tackled by overzealous security guards on this occasion), flowers in hand, and headed to Svetlana's nearest metro station which was located far in the east of Moscow. From here, I got a taxi to her apartment to pick her up, as requested (or rather, demanded). She was visibly delighted with the flowers and we both got into the taxi ready for our hour long journey to the centre of Moscow.

Now, an hour long journey at the beginning of a first date is awkward enough when you both speak the same first language. It is even more so when one of you (in this case, me) is required to speak in a second language. I tried my few well-worn and tested jokes which unfortunately did not seem to translate well into Russian on this occasion. So, out of jokes, I resorted to the typical small talk one might expect one a first date such as hobbies, work etc. During a brief lull in the conversation, we discussed our respective days and she informed me that she had spent the majority of the day cleaning her apartment which she shared with her aunt. I replied, jokingly, that cleaning is boring. With a look of almost disgust on her face she asked me if I liked living in filth to which I replied obviously not. She could not seem to fathom that someone could dislike cleaning but still partake in the activity out of hygienic necessity.

An hour later, we arrived at a delightful little bistro. After checking in our coats, we were taken to our table on the second floor. Svetlana was ecstatic with the choice of restaurant and I was feeling fairly pleased with myself. The food was delicious and, as we became more comfortable in each other's company, the conversation began to flow. The only brief hairy moment was when I almost ordered a dessert containing nuts. When I ordered dessert I asked whether it contained nuts and received the reply "чуть-чуть" (pronounced choot choot) which means 'some/a little'. For some unknown reason, I almost proceeded with the order until I realised that 'some' nuts could still probably kill me. As the evening drew to a close, I ordered Svetlana a taxi and we went our separate ways, promising to see each other again. All in all, it had been a rather successful date.

The following week, Svetlana and I had our second date. Again, I took responsibility for the arrangements, and this time I decided to pull out all the stops. We would start by going up the Ostankino Television Tower which offered panoramic views of Moscow, followed by a meal at a sushi restaurant. Despite this being our second date, I did not dare raise the prospect of meeting at a metro station and so, like before, there were taxis galore. Keen to avoid what turned out to be a non-existent queue, I had booked tickets online for the Television Tower. Compared to the price of tourist attractions in London, these were not prohibitively expensive but still more expensive than usual at £15.00 each. I should add that, in Russia, it is customary for the man to pay for everything, at least for the first few dates.

Prior to leaving my apartment in a mad rush, I realised that I had forgotten to print off our tickets for the Television Tower. It was when I printed off said tickets that I saw that there was a problem. The entrance date for the tickets was the following day. I realised that I had two options. Firstly, I could pretend that this was intentional and that the idea was to have a romantic evening of stargazing under the Tower in temperatures of -15 degrees Celsius, until the following day. Secondly, I could buy another pair of tickets. I opted for the latter.

So, stressed, late and down another £30.00 I dashed out of the apartment. Again, I would be picking up Svetlana from her apartment before getting another taxi to take us to the Television Tower, followed by a further taxi to take us to a restaurant. Although relatively cheap, I couldn't help but think that this taxi situation was getting a little out of hand. Upon arrival at the Tower we had to go through security which, as is usually the case in Russia, seemed slightly excessive. For our second date, I had bought a small box of chocolates for Svetlana. When we got to security she was advised that she would need to take these to a separate building for safe keeping. She was visibly frustrated at having to again put on her coat and leave security, only to return several minutes later. It wasn't my fault that the security guards were concerned the chocolates contained hand grenades, I thought.

After the rigmarole of security, we were eventually allowed access to the Television Tower which offered spectacular views of Moscow at night. After spending more than an hour here we headed to a central sushi restaurant I had chosen. Again the conversation seemed to flow extremely well, especially given the fact that I had spent the past few hours speaking entirely in Russian. The fact that I wasn't just uttering random gibberish (or at least Svetlana was kind enough not to mention this) was an achievement in itself. At the end of the night we said our goodbyes and promised to meet each other again shortly.

I will admit that, whilst I thoroughly enjoyed Svetlana's company, the financial implications and endless taxis were starting to take their toll. When discussing my latest date with my Russian teacher she informed me that, whilst it may be customary to pay for meals etc. on the first few dates, paying for endless taxis across the city is not. With this advice ringing in my ears, I contacted Svetlana and asked her to message me when she would like to next meet up, letting her take the initiative on this occasion. Following this, I would carefully broach the subject of using the metro for our next date. At the time of writing, I am still waiting to hear from Svetlana.

## 'WHY ARE YOU GOING THERE?'

*Walking*

In stark contrast to my dates with Svetlana, my most recent date, with a woman I will call Julia, did not involve any taxis or indeed any form of transport. Instead, and to my dismay, we essentially ended up doing a half marathon. Julia and I had again met online via a popular dating app. She was an interesting and intelligent woman who worked as a Chemistry teacher. At the very least, I hoped that I might be able to get some tips for my Science lessons. These were starting to result in increasingly more dangerous explosions in a desperate attempt to keep the children entertained.

Having exchanged several messages via the dating app, we agreed to meet up. Again, I was responsible for making the arrangements. With summer fast approaching, I thought that it might be nice to do something which would take advantage of the warm weather. My housemate had recently given me a leaflet for a relatively new cable car located in a leafy area of the city which is home to Moscow State University. The cable car travelled across the Moscow River. I booked two tickets, and told Julia to meet me at the metro station which wins the prize of most difficult to pronounce in Moscow: Vorobyovy Gory (воробьёвы горы). I did not reveal my plans so as to create an element of surprise.

111

## 'WHY ARE YOU GOING THERE?'

We met on what was a delightfully sunny Saturday afternoon. After exchanging pleasantries, we began our search for the cable car which, it turned out, was quite a hike from the metro station, thus marking the commencement of our marathon. Despite wearing high heels, Julia was still considerably more nimble on her feet than I. When we eventually reached the entrance to the cable car there was a large queue. Julia went to speak to the member of the staff at the front who motioned for us to skip the queue. I initially thought that this was just one of the many perks of my status as an Instagram celebrity (see Chapter III). However, I soon realised that it was simply because I had bought tickets in advance. Having skipped the queue, we got into one of the cable cars which promptly took us across the Moscow River. The views were, as ever, spectacular. However, the journey was incredibly short, lasting a total of five minutes. "What now?" I thought.

After disembarking, we found ourselves across the river from Moscow State University in an equally leafy area. "Let's walk, I like walking", said Julia when I asked her what she would like to do next. Or at least this is what I thought she said as she power walked a hundred metres in front of me. For the next few hours we walked along the Moscow River and the surrounding area. We would stop briefly (usually at my request) for a short break. However, after a few minutes sat on a bench, I was told to get up as it was time to continue our journey. Eventually, having worked up quite an appetite, we headed to a restaurant to get a bite to eat. This offered a welcome respite from walking. Again, despite taking place entirely in Russian, the conversation seemed to be going well.

After a nice meal, I thought that perhaps the evening was drawing to a natural close. I was wrong. Julia informed me that she would like to go for another 'short' walk. We ended up in St Petersburg. So, maybe this is a slight exaggeration but we did end up walking for another two hours by which point I was exhausted. It was survival of the fittest and I was clearly not fit. The company was great and the conversation enjoyable but it was hard to focus at times as I tried to catch my breath. I had done so many steps that day that the personal assistant on my phone, Alisa (Russia's version of Siri), seemed genuinely concerned, asking me if everything was OK. At around ten o'clock, our marathon was complete and we said our goodbyes.

Following our date, we remained in contact with a view to seeing each other again (hopefully something more sedentary). However, unfortunately, like walking, Julia had rather high expectations of me when it came to the frequency of our messaging.

## 'WHY ARE YOU GOING THERE?'

If I had not replied to a message within an hour she would become frustrated. On one such occasion, I had not replied to a message for a couple of hours because I had been working. Before I had had chance to reply she wrote "очень прятно" (pronounced ochen priyatna) which translates as 'nice to meet you'. This sounded fairly final so I asked her what was wrong. She answered that I was obviously too busy for her. I explained that I had been working so hadn't had chance to reply to her message but to no avail. I decided at this point that perhaps I was not the man for Julia.

# 'WHY ARE YOU GOING THERE?'

# VIII.

## Tula

### *Gingerbread, Guns and Dancing*

#### *The Mystery of the page four cat*

With summer fast approaching and another public holiday on the horizon (the particular public holiday on this occasion eludes me), my company decided to organise a weekend trip to a city called Tula. This city is located just over two hours south of Moscow and is known for two things: samovars and gingerbread. For those who are not aware, a samovar is a traditional metal container used to heat and boil water when making tea. In addition, Tula is well known for a specific type of gingerbread which is called priyanik (пряник) and contains a delicious fruit filling. Partial to the occasional (by this I mean daily) sweet treat, I did not have to think too long about whether to join my colleagues on this trip.

So, on a Saturday morning, around fifteen of us met at a central Moscow train station, ready for a new adventure. After boarding the train, I couldn't help but notice that a few of my colleagues already seemed slightly worse for wear, having partaken in a few alcoholic beverages. Little did I know that this was to set the tone for the remainder of the day. I decided that I would delay my participation in the alcoholic festivities until later that evening. As a general rule: if I can still taste my cornflakes, it's too early for beer. I find this to be a good rule of thumb.

Whilst we were on the train, a colleague handed us all a copy of a four page plan/ itinerary for the weekend. Four pages seemed slightly excessive, especially for my drunken colleagues who, it seemed, would struggle with reading four words at this point. Nevertheless, as someone had painstakingly gone to the trouble of writing this, the least I could do was give it a brief read. After reading a short history of Tula, I then read about the plan for the weekend. We would start by visiting some arms museums (arms as in weapons, not mutilated body parts), as well as the Kremlin. This would be followed by a trip to the gingerbread museum and an evening meal. It all seemed very civilised and pleasant.

Satisfied with what I had read, I turned over to the last page, only to be faced with a picture of a large cat. All of sudden, I found myself rather confused. Would we be going to a cat museum? Or, would we perhaps be staying in a cattery? This was probably still more conventional than the monastery where Lali and I had stayed in Rostov. I assumed that the cat had some significance but to this day I still do not know the meaning of the page four cat. I can only assume that the author inserted this clip art image in a delirious trance, after spending too long sat at his/her desk.

After arriving in Tula, we all crammed onto a public bus which would take us to a nearby hostel where we would be staying. The fellow passengers seemed somewhat bemused by our invasion. The fact that a large number of the group were speaking English also seemed to cause a stir. Despite only being several hours away from Moscow, it seems that the locals were not used to hearing English. In fact, whenever a colleague and I were speaking in English during the weekend, I would notice looks of curiosity and interest from passers-by. A mere fifteen minutes later we arrived at the hostel where we would be staying the night. After unpacking, and having a little lunch, it was time to head to the arms museum.

# 'WHY ARE YOU GOING THERE?'

## *Alcohol and guns: a deadly combination*

After a brief lunch, we headed out to the Kremlin which was also home to Tula's arms museum. Located a short distance from our hostel we headed out as a group down Tula's main street: Lenin Prospect. Like most 'Lenin Prospects', the street led to a statue of the man himself. Now, I have seen quite a few Lenin statues since being in Russia. By and large, these are all remarkably similar as you might expect. However, it was hard to escape the fact that, compared to other Lenins, 'Tula Lenin' is slightly on the chubby side. I put this down to an over indulgence in the local infamous gingerbread.

After a short stroll, we arrived at the Kremlin which, as is usually the case in Russia, was breathtaking. After admiring the view, and taking some photographs for Instagram, it was time to head to the arms museum. As we reached the museum my manager asked me if I would like a drink, waving a bottle of unknown cheap spirit in my direction. I politely declined. I felt that entering a building containing hundreds or thousands of different weapons whilst under the influence of alcohol was probably not the smartest idea. He simply shrugged and we headed inside.

## 'WHY ARE YOU GOING THERE?'

Now, what hadn't been explained on page 2 of the plan was that, once inside the museum, we were to dash around as if we were contestants on Dale Winton's *Supermarket Sweep*. After no more than ten minutes, a colleague and I received panicked phone calls from the others, asking where we were as they were leaving. Don't get me wrong; having already seen a large amount of guns, I'll admit that the novelty was starting to wear off. However, I had paid a 500 roubles entry fee and intended to get my money's worth. As the others left in search of alcohol, a colleague (Brian) and I continued our tour of the museum. In the final room, we ended up speaking to an old lady who worked in the museum. After our conversation, I was persuaded to complete a short survey which was interesting given that I didn't understand half of the questions. When asked what I would like to see more of in the museum I simply wrote 'more guns'. What else was there to say about an arms museum?

It was towards the end of our conversation that our new friend dropped an almighty bombshell. "Are you going to see the other arms museum?" she asked us. Up until this point we had been unaware that there was another museum. She explained that the 500 rouble entry fee included entry to two museums, the second of which was considerably larger and more impressive. She explained that all we needed to do was show our same ticket upon entry. It was at this point that we realised we did not have said ticket. Our manager had bought a ticket for us and had taken this with him on our departure. I had probably seen more than enough weapons for today but, nevertheless, I felt robbed. We bid farewell to our new friend and headed in search of a burger and beer to drown our sorrows.

## *Dancing*

A few hours, and several hundred calories later, we decided that we should probably contact the others to see where they were. Eventually, we received a reply, telling us to meet them at a bar near Lenin. Ten minutes later we arrived to meet our colleagues who, by now, were well and truly drunk. Upon arrival, I saw my manager slumped on a bar stool in a seemingly drunken stupor. "Did you go to the second museum?" he slurred. "It was much better than the first one", he proclaimed. "No, we didn't because you had our ticket", I replied with a hint of frustration. Lacking capacity for further conversation, he simply replied "oh" and returned to his drink. Feeling left behind, Brian and I decided to order some drinks in a perhaps hopeless attempt to catch up with the others.

## 'WHY ARE YOU GOING THERE?'

A few drinks later, I found myself awkwardly dancing, swaying my hips back and forth, and replicating the same dance moves which had proven so successful in Moscow. What was strange was that the venue was neither a bar nor a restaurant but rather something in between. With no proper dance floor to speak of people simply began dancing in between tables to Russian pop 'classics' as other guests were eating. It was all rather odd. However, I did not let the disgruntled stares of a young couple who were tucking into their borscht as I swayed nearby, deter me.

As the early hours of the morning approached, it was time to head home. As usual, there were several indicators that the night was over. The first indicator was that, in a drunken stupor, my manager took the novel approach of urinating in the street *towards*, as opposed to away from, oncoming traffic. Luckily for him, his aim was poor. I was, however, curious to know how a Russian driver would respond to his car being urinated on. Secondly, some of the group had booked an apartment rather than 'slumming' it in a hostel. They suggested that we continue the party back there. However, with them unable to remember in which direction they lived, I took the executive decision to head home for a much needed sleep.

# 'WHY ARE YOU GOING THERE?'

## *Gingerbread and Hide and Seek*

The next morning, I woke up nice and early feeling remarkably refreshed. As the others slept, Brian and I headed out in search of the infamously delicious priyanik for which Tula was known. Inside the Kremlin we headed into a shop which advertised itself as providing the best gingerbread in Tula. Faced with more gingerbread than I knew existed, I panicked. The cashier could smell this panic and pounced like an bloodthirsty Rottweiler. I ended up buying two slabs of gingerbread, each of which were the size of my face, as well as some other kind of sweet bread. One of the gingerbread slabs would be a present for a friend I told myself as I left the shop. However, aware of my gluttonous tendencies, I felt somewhat unconvinced.

As we arrived back at the hostel, it was eerily quiet. At first, we thought that perhaps our colleagues had all gone out for breakfast and would return shortly. However, upon further examination, I realised that all the bags were also missing which was strange. With our train in less than an hour, we decided to speak to the hotel receptionist who confirmed that the rest of the group had checked out some time ago. I checked my phone. I had not received a single message or call. Neither had Brian. It was at this point that we found ourselves in an extreme game of hide and seek with less than sixty minutes to catch our train out of Tula. Funnily enough, that we would be abandoned in an unfamiliar city hours away from Moscow had not been mentioned in the plan either. Upon reflection, perhaps this information should have taken priority over a large picture of a cat on page 4.

Not entirely confident in our sense of direction, we ordered a taxi which swiftly took us to the train station, with plenty of time to spare. Shortly afterwards, the rest of the group arrived. As we explained our confusion regarding the check-out process, we were met with vacant stares. Perhaps everyone else had a different version of the plan, I thought to myself. However, I would not let this ruin what had overall been a good weekend. As I sat on the train, I found myself fantasizing about the delicious gingerbread which would undoubtedly constitute my dinner. Did I really need to give the second slab of gingerbread to a friend, I thought to myself.

# 'WHY ARE YOU GOING THERE?'

# IX.

# Cyprus

## *Little Russia*

*Church of Saint Lazarus, Larnaca*

## 'WHY ARE YOU GOING THERE?'

### *Making plans for summer*

With the academic year drawing to a close, my thoughts started to turn to summer. My schools would all be closed during summer and my current teaching contract expired at the end of May. Unless I made plans, and quickly, I faced three months of living in the UK with my mum and sister. I would have no car or job, and little sanity come September. As much as I loved my family, this was clearly not an option.

One option was to do a summer camp. This entailed living and working with children for as little as two weeks or up to a total of three months. My company offered such summer camps, working with other organisations based in and around Moscow. This work offered a much needed income during the lean summer months. However, these camps did not have glowing reviews. Apparently, after agreeing to do such camps, you were essentially shipped off to some industrial estate in the middle of nowhere, hours away from Moscow. Once there, you found yourself stranded with dozens of children who looked to you as their sole source of entertainment for the entire time. This role was paid. However, given that there was nothing for miles around, aside from a few elderly ladies pedaling their wares on the street, the money was pretty useless. So, given what I had heard, I was fairly reluctant to sign up.

My suspicions were heightened when I went into the office one day, only to be bombarded by the member of staff in charge of organising these camps. "Elliot, we need your help, would you be able to do one of the camps this summer?", he asked me with a nervous twitch in his eye. I told him I would think about it. An hour or so later, as I was leaving the office, the same member of staff came up to me again. "Elliot, I forgot to mention, but we're running low on teachers this year, so if you could do as many camps as possible, that would be great".

There was an air of desperation in his voice which I found unsettling and which only reaffirmed my fears. I told him that I would let him know, which, as any fellow Brit knows, is code for: no way in hell. Sure enough, my colleague and friend found himself at one of these camps in the middle of nowhere. There was no reliable internet and his only source of company was Coco the cat. However, it was not all bad. After some negotiations, he managed to get his sentence reduced by two weeks.

Deciding against these camps, I still had no plans for summer. Aware of this, during a lesson, my Russian teacher made a suggestion. She had a friend who was a director of a private language school on the outskirts of Moscow. Every year, this school ran a two week summer camp in Cyprus. The position was voluntary but everything (aside from the costs of one flight) would be covered. If I wanted, she could give my contact details to this friend and see if there was still space. Enthused by the prospect of sea and sun for two weeks, I agreed. One or two weeks later, I received a phone call from a Russian woman named Galina who provided me with more information about the camp and asked me whether I was interested. Despite having never met this woman, I agreed.

### 'This is not a holiday"

Several months later, I eventually met up with Galina and the rest of the team with whom I would be travelling to Cyprus. We met at Galina's school which was on the outskirts of Moscow. This journey constituted my first use of Moscow's commuter trains, affectionately known as 'electrichkas' (электри́чка). As is usually the case, my journey on public transport was not entirely uneventful. In a rush, I had bought a ticket for an 'ordinary' train (обычный). However, unbeknown to me, there was also an 'express' train which was all of ten minutes quicker. Of course, I managed to get on the only express train at the station, with my 'ordinary' ticket.

## 'WHY ARE YOU GOING THERE?'

No one checked my ticket during the journey. However, upon arrival, my ticket would not scan. A member of staff angrily told me that I had bought the wrong ticket and would need to 'upgrade' it to an express ticket, which I did. To this day, I still have no idea how the machine could tell that I had been on an express train in the first place. Various trains (both ordinary and express) were coming into the station from Moscow at the same time. Maybe it was the smug look on my face after saving ten minutes on my journey which gave me away.

After eventually being waved through, now with both an ordinary and express ticket in hand, I was met by a young woman called Kate. She worked at Galina's school as an English teacher and would also be coming to Cyprus. Running late, we briskly walked to the school for our meeting. Upon arrival, I was warmly greeted by Galina and her colleague Marina. After exchanging brief pleasantries, we got down to business. Galina handed me a two page plan covering the two week trip. After a brief perusal of said plan, it was clear that this was no holiday. Each day was jam packed with different activities to keep the children occupied. There would be twenty three children, whose lives would be in our hands for the next two weeks.

## 'WHY ARE YOU GOING THERE?'

Although this sounded daunting, I was promised that there would be plenty of sea and sun. The plan was much better than the plan for Tula. However, sadly, there was the regrettable reoccurrence of clip art. For example, for Tuesday, there was just a big picture of a London double Decker bus. "Jesus. A trip to London. That will be a long day", I thought to myself. Seeing my confusion, Galina explained that this picture just meant that we would be going on an excursion. I can't help but wonder whether sometimes, in the absence of ideas, people just grab a picture from clip art and hope for the best. Perhaps Theresa May's private Brexit plans just consisted of various images of cats? This would explain a lot. Clip art aside, I felt fairly reassured by what I had been told and was ready to go to Cyprus.

### *Day One: A Treasure Hunt*

The day had finally arrived. After weeks of planning and preparation I found myself waiting at Vnukovo Airport in Moscow, ready to board a plane to Larnaca in Cyprus. This would be my first time in Cyprus. However, unfortunately, any excitement was overwhelmed by my sheer tiredness. I had only had four hours sleep the previous night and this was on a bare mattress with no bedding. As there was no guarantee that I would be returning to the same apartment in September, I needed to pack up all my things and store them for the summer. This was not easy as I had, by now, accumulated three suitcases worth of belongings.

Thankfully, my friend let me store my things at her apartment for the entire summer which was a great help. I had also essentially done a marathon around Moscow the day before, visiting various areas of the city (before you ask, no, I had not had another date with Julia). After around half an hour of waiting, I was met by Kate    at the airport. We then waited for two children who we would be travelling with us on the same flight: Lena and Dima. We would be like a little family. The rest of the group would be coming on a much later flight that evening.

After a few minor hurdles (various documents were required given that Lena and Dima were not our children and would be travelling without parents), we breezed through security and eventually boarded the plane for our flight. The flight was rather uneventful other than the fact that I spent the next four hours sat next to a woman wearing a cheetah eye mask. Occasionally we would lock eyes as her head rolled towards me whilst she slept, which was slightly unnerving, but all in all the flight was fine. After disembarking, the heat hit me straight away. Moscow had been warm, but not like this. It was nice but perhaps two weeks later I would take a different view. After entering the airport we queued up to go through passport control. After five minutes of queuing, I hastily decided to abandon my new family, heading to the desk for 'EU Citizens', proudly waving my passport in the air. I will miss this perk once we leave the EU.

After being reunited with my new family, we got into a taxi which took us to our hotel. The receptionist, aware of our group's imminent arrival, provided the four of us with a room whilst we awaited the rest of the group. After grabbing some lunch, Kate and I then had the almighty task of keeping these children entertained for the next six or so hours. We started off by playing the game UNO but already there were problems. "I want to swim in the pool", proclaimed Lena. It was around midday and ferociously hot. "No, it's too hot. Maybe later", replied Kate. Lena proceeded to stare at me, eyes full of expectation. I realised that, at this point, there were two options. First, I could be a supportive partner and simply agree with Kate. Second, I could play the role of the 'cool' father and let her swim, but undoubtedly face an argument later that evening when Lena was a red as a lobster. I opted for the prior.

## 'WHY ARE YOU GOING THERE?'

An hour or so later (UNO starts to lose its novelty after twenty minutes), we had a brief break, before relinquishing to Lena's repeated requests and headed to the rooftop pool. This was the first time I saw Lena smile. Later on, we headed to the beach which was a few minutes' walk from the hotel. The beach was beautiful and, as the sun shone down on me, I was sure I had made the right choice in coming here.

Upon return to the hotel, I asked Kate for the keys to my suitcase. I had given these to her earlier in the day for safekeeping. After some frantic searching through her bag, she announced that she couldn't find them. At first, I thought this was a joke. During our meeting back in Moscow, Galina had said that we would need to prepare a treasure hunt for the children during the two weeks. So, naturally, I thought that Kate was just trying to get in some much needed practice beforehand. I played along for a while, joining in with the 'search' for my keys.

However, after around ten minutes, and seeing the panicked look on Kate's face, I realised that perhaps this was not a practice treasure hunt after all. Unfortunately, inside my suitcase were my passport, wallet, phone and all other valuable items. Unable to open my suitcase, I would find myself in the position of a contestant on Bear Grylls' *The Island.* For those not aware, this is a British TV show where contestants are left stranded on a desert island with nothing but their clothes and some survival gear. Maybe this analogy is a slight exaggeration but, either way, it was far from ideal.

Resigning myself to the fact that the keys were lost forever, I headed down to reception with my suitcase to see whether they could help. Given that it was now late evening, no one from the maintenance team was available and so they suggested that I head to a nearby shop up the road instead. At this exact moment, the rest of the group (who were annoyingly cheerful) arrived at the hotel. "Hey, how are you?" asked Galina in an upbeat voice. "I've been better. I've lost the keys to my suitcase", I muttered before heading to the local shop. When we arrived at the shop, I explained to the elderly couple what had happened. The man proceeded to get a hammer from the back of his shop to try and break open the lock.

Kate and I spent the next twenty minutes watching this man attack my suitcase with a hammer. It could have been worse, I thought to myself. He could have been attacking me with a hammer for bothering him with such nonsense late at night. Eventually, and just as I was about to give up hope, the lock popped open. I gratefully thanked the owners and promised to return the following day to buy a new padlock.

# 'WHY ARE YOU GOING THERE?'

Kate and I wearily returned to the hotel, ready for some dinner, followed by a good night's sleep. As we stood outside the room, I asked Kate for the room key. She promptly reached inside her bag. After a few minutes of fumbling, I saw the same panic stricken look which I recognised from earlier. "You cannot be serious", I said in my best John McEnroe impression. "Can we not just leave the treasure hunt until Day 2, at least?" I thought to myself. Having lost a second set of keys in less than one hour, Kate ran back to the local shop which we had just left. She sheepishly returned several minutes later, keys in hand. "I will take these", I announced. I would be assuming the role of key holder from now on.

Stressed, we headed to a local restaurant, where the rest of the group had already started eating. Galina frantically rang us, saying that if we didn't hurry up, we would miss our meal. Normally, I would be devastated at the prospect of missing a meal. However, this evening was different. Aside from my sheer exhaustion, the restaurant where we were to head had the rather unfortunate name of 'Panos'. For those who don't know Russian, the word 'Panos' (понос), translates as diarrhoea. This was the last thing I needed, after what had already been a draining day. I must admit, I was slightly surprised by the choice of name given the amount of

Russian tourists which Cyprus welcomes each year. I heard so much Russian during my time here that I nicknamed the island 'Little Russia'.

Anyway, against all odds, my bowels were fine. I should add that, during this meal, Kate opened her bag to reveal my 'lost' suitcase keys which had inadvertently stuck to a magnetic clip. Tired, and nervously picking at my meal in a restaurant named after a bowel disorder, I was unable to see the funny side at the time. Once back at the hotel I collapsed onto my bed, nervous for what the next day might bring. I slept with my keys that night.

### *Pizza on the roof*

One lesson I learnt during my two weeks with children in Cyprus was that, in order for you to get a good night's sleep; you need to tire them out, almost to the point of unconsciousness. The moment they are bored (even for a matter of minutes), they will invariably start running around and/or setting fire to things. One of the ways we kept the children entertained during the evening was via the now infamous 'Pizza Party'. The hotel where we were staying had a rooftop pool which, by and large, was quiet during the evening. Aware that food is always a good way to bribe children, we would order seven or eight boxes of pizza which would be delivered to the rooftop. Following this, there would be a 'disco'. Perhaps unsurprisingly, things did not always go to plan.

For example, the first 'Pizza Party' took place one or two days after our arrival in Cyprus and so, the children were inevitably excited. I headed to the rooftop slightly before seven o'clock to await the pizza delivery. Galina had asked me to go up earlier to ensure that the greedier children didn't get carried away with the pizza whilst the other children were absent. I took great pride in my role as Pizza Officer. In particular, I thoroughly enjoyed telling the children that they had to wait for the others before eating as I stuffed my face with a slice of pepperoni pizza. The 'pizza' part of the 'Pizza Party' went fine. It was the 'party' which was problematic. After consuming thousands of calories in pizza, the children were expected to dance to some pop classics and at least pretend to enjoy themselves.

The first party was a slight anti-climax given that it was only the adults who were 'dancing'. Some of the children inevitably felt they were too cool for this and instead chose to glue themselves to their phones. The other children were perhaps a little nervous given that they had only met one another one or two days before. Understandably, they did not fancy doing the Macarena with complete strangers. Perhaps wanting to put everyone out of their misery, our water-loving friend Lena decided to take drastic action. All of a sudden, after a torturous hour of 'dancing', there was an almighty splash. Naturally, everyone stopped dancing to see what had happened. After a few seconds we saw the bobbing head of a fully clothed Lena in the swimming pool. Apparently she had 'fallen' into the pool but, given the smile on her face, it was hard to avoid the conclusion that this was intentional. With that, Galina grimly announced that the first Pizza Party was over.

Thankfully, as the weeks progressed, the pizza parties did seem to improve to the point where even Lena seemed to be having a good time. In addition to my role as Pizza Officer, I also settled nicely into my second role as resident DJ. Using my phone and a Bluetooth speaker I would boom out a wide variety of pop classics. However, using YouTube, it was perhaps inevitable that I would stumble upon some outlandish videos. Sure enough, during the second or third Pizza Party (there were four in total), I came across 'the chicken song'. This was a type of techno song (I know), accompanied by the sound of a chicken. I initially played this as a joke but amongst several children this became a firm favourite as they ran around the pool pretending to be a chicken. I did also come across a ten hour remix version of this song but this felt slightly excessive. Overall, I would say that the pizza parties were a success. However, one unexpected result is that I now find myself unable to indulge in a pepperoni pizza unless it is accompanied by 'the chicken song'.

### *Barking Mad*

Compared to the children I have taught at Barvikha and 'the Bear Pit', the children in Cyprus were delightful. However, as with all the children I have met during my time in Russia, they too had their own quirks. There were two girls in particular who were quirkier than most. The first of these girls I will call Diana. Diana was a pocket-sized girl of around eight or nine years old. She was accompanied on the trip by her older sister. For whatever reason, Diana seemed to take a liking to me and so we got to know each other fairly well during the two weeks. For the majority of the day, she was delightful. However, when it was time to swim in the sea she turned into a devil child.

Every day, between four and six o'clock in the afternoon, we would take the children to the beach to swim in the sea. Our primary role as team leaders was to ensure that the children didn't drown to death. Compared to my friend who was continuing to serve out his sentence in the middle of nowhere, several hours of 'working' in the warm Cypriot sea perhaps doesn't sound so bad.

However, this is misleading. As soon as we got in the sea, Diana would make a beeline for me. After momentarily dipping underwater, Jaws music would begin to play as she slowly emerged with a clump of wet sand in her hand. She would then proceed to throw this in my direction. Afterwards, in a menacing and thick Russian accent, she would ask: "Elliot, did you like my present?" This would be followed by an equally sinister giggle. She would then dip underwater and the process would start again. This would continue for two hours. On one occasion, I made the mistake of picking Diana up in the air and throwing her in the sea, in the hope that this would deter her. Instead, she loved this, as did the other children. That afternoon, I found myself throwing twenty three children into the sea one by one. By the end of the day, I could not feel my arms.

Another girl who was equally as quirky was Natasha. She was of a similar age to Diana and was here with her brother and mum. Now, for the majority of the trip, Natasha behaved fairly normally. Well, as normal as can be expected for a child of her age. However, during the second week, I noticed a change in her behaviour. In particular, she became more feral. This all started fairly inconspicuously enough when, one morning, instead of saying hello she simply barked at me. I naively assumed that this was just a phase which would last no more than a few hours. I was wrong. Five days later I was at my wits end and ended up shouting on the middle of the beach: "Stop barking!" to which she proceeded to bark. In between barks she would growl which was perhaps more unnerving. What was strange was that with other human beings she was a perfectly friendly dog. In fact, she would just whimper at Kate who would proceed to stroke her head.

The barking reached its peak at the final Pizza Party, culminating in a fourteen second barking session. For these fourteen seconds, Natasha barked at me in time to the music. At the end, she completed the session with a wolf howl which offered a terrifying glimpse into the next stage of her development. Luckily, by the time the wolf stage reached its peak, I was far away back in Moscow. For those who might not believe me, I have a fourteen second video as evidence. I sent said video to my friend who was also a teacher in Moscow. He was fairly unphased by this, which perhaps says a lot about our profession. I am currently campaigning for this video to be mandatory viewing for individuals who are considering a career which involves working with children.

# 'WHY ARE YOU GOING THERE?'

### *'This is the last last dish'*

*'Food glorious food': the never-ending meal at a restaurant Cyprus.*

After long days of being surrounded by children, Kate and I found it essential to have some time to ourselves in the evening. We would usually be let free around nine or ten o'clock, whereupon we would dash to the nearest restaurant in search of food and alcohol. After two weeks, I couldn't help but notice the glaring differences between customer service in Russia and Cyprus.

## 'WHY ARE YOU GOING THERE?'

In Russia, customer service is very transactional and direct. Upon entering a café or restaurant you are usually met with a grim stare followed by the question: "What do you want?" You then proceed to order your meal which is promptly brought to you by the waiter or waitress. At the end of the meal, you ask for the bill by shouting across the room: 'molodoy chelovek' (молодой человек) or 'devushka' (девушка) which translates as 'young man' or 'young woman' respectively. Following this, you pay your meal and leave. It is not service with a smile but it is prompt and efficient.

Personally, I find it annoying when in a shop or restaurant a smiling member of staff asks me about my day or my plans, pretending to actually care. I have come here to buy some milk and bread, not tell you my life story. Also, if we're honest, you don't really care what I am going to do after purchasing said items but you have been told to ask me by your boss. Overall, I find that the Russian no nonsense style of customer service rather suits me.

What I quickly learnt was that customer service in Cyprus could not be more different. Now, I am fully aware that, as a tourist destination, waiters and waitresses have to make the extra effort to entice customers. However, this aside, the waiters and waitresses were extremely friendly and genuinely seemed happy to see us. Initially, this was a refreshing change from Russia. However, it soon began to wear thin.

For example, one evening we went to a quaint restaurant located on a side street in Larnaca. We sat outside on the street as live music was playing. The atmosphere was great. A smiling, bubbly, waiter came over to us, promptly taking our order. Having already eaten, we just ordered some wine. Or so we thought. Something had evidently gotten lost in translation as ten minutes later, the same waiter brought out a mezze consisting of around twenty five dishes. As someone who enjoys his food, this was a happy accident. The food was the best I had eaten in Cyprus.

However, in a bizarre game of cat and mouse, each time we finished a dish, it would be replaced by another. In a barefaced lie a waitress informed us that she had brought what was the 'last dish'. However, this was promptly followed by what our waiter promised us was the 'last last dish'. This too was a lie as he later brought us dessert. However, being lied to in an attempt to serve us *more* food was a welcome change from Rostov. We could not keep up and by the end we had to accept defeat and take the remainder home.

## 'WHY ARE YOU GOING THERE?'

However, it was not until we sought to obtain the bill that the true differences in customer service became obvious. Unable to simply shout 'Young man' across the restaurant, as in Russia, we patiently waited to catch the waiter's attention. Eventually, we managed to catch his eye and he came over promising to bring the bill shortly. Twenty minutes later, we had still not received the bill. I looked inside the restaurant to see where our waiter had disappeared. Upon doing so, to my horror, I saw him dancing to the live music, as other diners gathered around him throwing napkins in the air. I thought I saw him throw our bill in the air as he span around but I could not be sure as I was too far away. Livid, I found the other waitress, who promptly brought our bill over and wished us goodnight. After this evening, I found myself longing for the Russian 'no frills' customer service.

# 'WHY ARE YOU GOING THERE?'

## *Talent Show and Goodbyes*

The finale of the summer camp was a talent show which took place on the final evening. The audience consisted of proud parents as well as teachers from the language centre where the children had been studying English each morning. Kate, I and the other teachers constituted the judging panel. To my surprise, the children (including the older ones) had taken this talent show incredibly seriously and had been rehearsing for the previous fortnight whenever they had a spare moment. Thus, I had high expectations and, thankfully, I was not disappointed. I saw everything from gymnastics and dancing to an impressive Powerpoint presentation on the workings of a computer. After much difficulty, we eventually decided on three winners. It was a delightful conclusion to what had been a thoroughly enjoyable albeit exhausting and sometimes bizarre two weeks.

The next morning Kate, Lena, Dima and I bid farewell to the rest of the group who were boarding a plane later that evening. I would say that I was looking forward to returning to Moscow. However, in fact, I would only be in Moscow for a total of seven hours before getting on a twelve hour train journey to a city called Petrozavodsk in the scenic region of Karelia located near the Finnish border. Nevertheless, I was excited to be returning to

## 'WHY ARE YOU GOING THERE?'

Russia. As I sat in my seat waiting for the plane to take off I looked to the left and saw my neighbour vigorously praying which was slightly unsettling. I knew that Russian airlines did not have a great reputation but were they really that bad, I thought to myself. Assuming that this woman knew better than I (as someone who was flying with a Russian airline for only the second time), I asked if I could join in with her prayers, proceeding to cross myself fervently.

# 'WHY ARE YOU GOING THERE?'

# X.

# Karelia

## *Cakes and Lakes*

*Europe's largest lake: Lake Ladoga in Karelia*

## 'WHY ARE YOU GOING THERE?'

After arriving back in Moscow, I immediately called my friend and told her that I would be heading over to her apartment shortly to collect my things. She had kindly agreed to store my possessions at her apartment during the summer months. Despite having just returned to Moscow after a sunny two weeks in Cyprus, there was no time to waste. That same evening, I was taking a train to a city called Petrozavodsk in the Republic of Karelia. It is known for its breathtaking scenery. In particular, Karelia is home to Europe's two largest lakes: Lake Ladoga and Lake Onego. In spite of my fatigue, I was excited to start the second leg of summer adventure.

### *Trying not to stand out*

After hurriedly collecting my things from my friend's apartment, I hopped into a taxi and headed to Moscow's Leningradskaya train station to begin my twelve hour journey to Petrozavodsk. This was the first time that I had taken an overnight train in Russia so I had no idea what to expect. Unfamiliar with the different class systems on Russian overnight trains, I had booked a seat in the 'Platskart' section of the train. This was considerably cheaper than other areas of the train.

## 'WHY ARE YOU GOING THERE?'

When I told my Russian friends beforehand that I would be travelling to Karelia by platskart they looked at me with pity. I was told that it would be 'intimate'. By this, they meant that it was crowded and that I should expect someone else's body parts in and around my face. Indeed, the platskart section of the train consists of an open sleeping compartment with bunk beds on either side of the carriage. To get to the top bunk there are steps which you need to climb upon and propel yourself upwards rather like a monkey. Having witnessed this now on several occasions, I can confirm that it is a skill which is only honed over many years of practice.

So, having got onto the train and found the correct carriage, I was keen to keep a low profile in an attempt to blend in with my fellow passengers. Sadly, this did not last long. When I found my place I was slightly concerned to find that my bed was positioned sideways mid-air. For at least several minutes, I found myself pulling on various levers in the vain hope that my bed would miraculously pop into position. Alas, this was not the case. After acquiring some spectators, I reluctantly asked for help and finally managed to get my bed into position, following which I collapsed in utter exhaustion. Relieved, I settled down in the hope that I would now be able to get some sleep.

## 'WHY ARE YOU GOING THERE?'

However, less than five minutes later the train conductor told me to get down as my bed was not secured properly. Apparently, the passenger below me was concerned that he would be crushed to death by my nine stone frame during the middle of the night. Eventually, after what had been around twenty minutes of fiddling around with my bed and making 'friends' with other passengers (by 'friends' I of course mean enemies), I settled down.

Despite my exhaustion and the rhythmic motion of the train, I did not sleep particularly well that night. So, feeling slightly worse for wear, the next morning I hopped down from my bed as gracefully as I could manage, to get myself a coffee. As I returned, coffee in hand, I prepared to make my way back up to the top bunk. The problem with the top bunk is that it is located so high up that you cannot sit upright so have no choice but to lie down. Thus, there was a high probability that I would end up spilling my coffee all over my shirt.

However, just as I was preparing to climb back up, my lower neighbour indicated that I could sit down on the edge of his bed instead, for which I was extremely grateful. Sipping my coffee and gazing out at the untamed Russian countryside, I felt content. This is exactly how I had imagined the 'real Russia', outside of Moscow. However, five minutes into my daydreaming (and only halfway through my coffee), I was tapped on the shoulder. My neighbour motioned that he wanted to lie down so I would need to return upstairs. My time was up.

## *Fights and Potholes*

Several hours later, I eventually arrived in Petrozavodsk. Aside from Karelia's reputation for a stunning nature, one of the reasons I had chosen to visit Petrozavodsk was because I had a friend who lived here with her family. We had begun communicating online as language partners on a popular website several years ago and had remained in touch ever since. More recently we had met up together in Moscow for the first time, following which I had agreed to come visit her and her family in Karelia. Banni often lamented the lack of customer service and manners among society in Russia. She said that she found people to be particularly rude where she lived. The 'directness' which I find so refreshing is perhaps seen differently through the eyes of a local.

Despite her warnings of the 'coldness' of people in the Russian north, I remained optimistic. That was, until I left the train station. As I waited outside the train station to be met by my friend, a heated argument erupted between two drivers in the car park. I was not sure what had triggered this argument or indeed the specifics of what was said but I knew enough Russian to realise that these two men were not on friendly terms. After five or so minutes, the argument came to an abrupt end and the two men went their separate ways. I thought I had heard the exchange of offensive remarks about each other's mothers, but I cannot be sure. As the two men left, I felt my initial optimism take a hit. Perhaps my friend was right after all, I thought. Shortly afterwards, I was met at the train station by the beaming smile of my friend.

We decided to head to a nearby restaurant for a bite to eat. She suggested a pan-Asian restaurant not far from the train station. The food was excellent and the prices were significantly lower than Moscow. It is true that, once you leave the capital, prices are often cut in half. However, it would be wrong to assume that the quality is also lower. In fact, I have had many experiences where the quality of food is better than what I have experienced in Moscow. Regrettably, amongst many tourists and also my colleagues who have not ventured outside of Moscow, there is a misguided assumption that leaving the capital is tantamount to leaving civilisation. However, what I have found is that, whilst there are fewer facilities and job opportunities, people who live outside of Moscow generally live a much more comfortable life than one imagines.

Following our meal, my friend guided me to the Airbnb apartment where I would be staying for the next three weeks. Indicative of the price differences, this apartment had cost me just shy of £350 for three weeks. As we headed to the apartment, she drew my attention to the state of the pavements and roads which were riddled with potholes. Indeed, I nearly lost my suitcase in the depths of these potholes on many occasions. Banni explained that in Petrozavodsk, they would 'repair' the pavements and roads on an annual basis. However, they would use the cheapest materials they could find, knowing that they would need repairing again in a year, hence guaranteeing future work. I should add that this is not a phenomenon limited to Petrozavodsk. Recently, the pavement leading to my local metro station was similarly 'repaired'. For several weeks, walking to the metro was tantamount to being a contestant on the Japanese game show 'Takeshi's Castle', such were the obstacles.

However, my friend has a wicked sense of humour and decided to make light of the situation by telling me a popular joke. "Elliot, in Russia we say that you can always tell a drunk driver from a sober one because the drunk driver will drive straight whereas the sober one will swerve to avoid the potholes". There is one thing I have noticed about the Russian people. In spite of any difficulties or adversities they may face, they will readily find a joke to lighten the mood.

## *'Our Englishman'*

During my three weeks in Karelia I vowed to experience everything that the region had to offer. This, quite predictably for those who know me, included lots of food. My friend's family own a popular Stolovaya (a Russian canteen) in the city which is known for its delicious, hearty food. After a few days of settling in, Banni took me to her Stolovaya and introduced me to her mother who has an equally wicked sense of humour and a broad smile on her face no matter the time of day or circumstances.

From this day onwards, *Stolovaya Number 8* in Petrozavodsk became my second home. The food was incredible and I would highly recommend this Stolovaya to anyone visiting the region. Like many Russian canteens the menu included Russian classics such as borscht and solyanka (another delicious soup). However, in addition to this, there was kharcho (a particularly tasty Georgian soup), Karelian pasties and much more. Nevertheless, having a sweet tooth, my personal favourite were the fresh homemade croissants filled with apricot jam which Banni's mother would bake several times a week. Aware of my love for these sweet treats, my friend would text me in advance to let me know when they would be ready which I always appreciated as I ran halfway across the city drooling at the mouth.

I set up camp at the Stolovaya over the next few weeks and became acquainted with many of the regular customers. Banni's mother would proudly introduce me as 'our Englishman'. One such customer was an elderly woman whose name I have sadly forgotten. One afternoon, this woman shuffled into the canteen and began speaking with her mother in a hushed voice, occasionally looking over in my direction. I was sat at a table with my friend and could hear this woman asking her mother who I was.

Later on, this woman approached us and introduced herself to me. She asked me a few cursory questions such as where I was from and my age. With that, and not feeling the need to ask any further questions, she decided that I would be a good partner for my friend and indicated that we should get married. I was slightly taken aback by the speed with which she came to this conclusion. Nevertheless, compared to the West, Russian society remains conservative and there is a pressure on women to marry young. Perhaps this woman was of the view that any husband was better than no husband hence the reason she didn't feel the need to ask me more probing questions such as whether I was a serial killer.

Afterwards, my friend said that this woman was slightly outspoken which I thought was an understatement. She explained that on one occasion she had bumped into this woman on this street and had had a brief chat with her. At the end of said conversation, the woman proceeded to inform my friend that she had a great bottom before heading off in the opposite direction. Regrettably, I never saw this woman again during my stay in Petrozavodsk.

# 'WHY ARE YOU GOING THERE?'

## *A day trip: Ruskeala and Valaam*

*The marble lake at Ruskeala Mountain Park, Karelia*

Nearing the end of my three weeks in Petrozavodsk, I realised that I had still not seen all of the beautiful nature which the region had to offer. Not knowing when I would return, I decided to book an excursion via a local tour operator. After considering the various options, I opted for a twelve hour round trip to Ruskeala and Valaam. The former is a Mountain Park at the heart of which is a stunning marble lake. The latter is an island situated in the northern portion of Lake Ladoga and is best known for its 14th Century monastery of the same name. Both are located several hours away from Petrozavodsk and can be quite difficult to reach so I was advised to book an organised tour.

On the morning of the tour, I woke up at five o'clock ready for what promised to be a long day. Bleary eyed, I headed to the meeting point for our group which was outside a local hotel. When I arrived, I was met by around twenty other people who were similarly congregating outside the hotel. I assumed that these would be my fellow travel companions for the day. Either that, or the hotel breakfast was being served *al fresco* this morning. Everyone apart from me was Russian and I was by far the youngest of the group.

Eventually, after around twenty minutes, a coach arrived which we were hurriedly ushered onto by our energetic and bubbly tour guide. Finding a spare two seats towards the back of the coach I settled down, hoping to enjoy a brief nap during the first leg of our five hour journey. However, almost immediately, I was accosted by a pair of older women who informed me that I was sat in their seats. How they had come to this conclusion (despite the fact that we had not reserved seats and there were plenty of other free spaces), I was not quite sure. Nevertheless, knowing that any protestation on my part would be futile, I simply sighed and moved seats. For the next few hours, I found myself alternating between sleep and admiring the vast and endless countryside out of the window.

After several hours, we finally reached our first destination: Ruskeala Mountain Park. We promptly disembarked from the coach and were provided with some fashionable wristbands, gaining us entry to the park. Following this, we were divided into smaller groups, each of which was provided with a tour guide who would lead us around the park. Our tour guide was dressed in traditional Karelian costume which consisted of a long-sleeved white blouse and a red and white long dress.

For the next hour or so, we were given a tour of the Mountain Park by our guide. The tour was in Russian so sadly I could not understand everything. Nevertheless, the main reason that I booked this tour was to appreciate the nature which was truly remarkable and, in any event, beyond words. At the heart of the park is a lake which is surrounded by gleaming marble cliffs. The tour guide took us around the entire perimeter of the lake, giving us the opportunity to admire the lake from all angles. With the sun shining and reflecting onto the rippling lake, it was difficult to imagine a more beautiful place.

# 'WHY ARE YOU GOING THERE?'

Following the conclusion of the tour, it was time to get back onto the coach for the second leg of our journey: Valaam. Valaam is an island situated in the northern portion of Lake Ladoga and is best known for its 14th Century monastery of the same name. Although I am not particularly religious, churches in Russia are stunning and well worth seeing. Like Ruskeala, Valaam is a major tourist attraction for visitors of this region. With it only being a stone's throw away (a mere couple of hours, which constitutes a 'stone's throw' in Russian terms) from Ruskeala, I had decided to add this onto my trip.

After several hours of driving, we boarded a boat which was extremely crowded. I found myself sat next to a monk and two women who had an innumerable amount of cherries. Upon arrival, we were met on the island by a shorter, energetic man with glasses and dark hair. This man was to be our tour guide for the afternoon. Like Ruskeala, the entire tour took place in Russian. However, unlike my previous tour guide, this man spoke extremely quickly and so it was very difficult at times to catch what was being said. After thirty minutes or so of attempting to understand the guide, I resigned myself to admiring the beautiful scenery instead.

## 'WHY ARE YOU GOING THERE?'

*View of Lake Ladoga from archipelago of Valaam*

Several hours later, our tour came to an end. Like my fellow passengers, I enthusiastically clapped the tour guide despite having no idea what he had said to me for the past few hours. I then hurriedly headed back to the agreed meeting point so as to not miss our boat. Despite having thoroughly enjoyed the trip, being stranded on an island inhabited only by monks, as friendly as they were, did not appeal to me. Thankfully, I made it back in time and, one hour later, I found myself back on the coach to Petrozavodsk. Utterly exhausted, I slept for the remainder of the journey. We arrived back around midnight, following which I stumbled back to my apartment ready to get some sleep. This was my final night in the apartment which I had called home for the past three weeks.

The next morning, I woke up and began packing my things in preparation for the next leg of my summer adventure: Nizhny Novgorod. I would be staying in this large Russian city for three weeks for a Russian language summer school. So, after checking out of my apartment, I (and a rather large suitcase) headed to *Stolovaya Number 8* for my final supper. Determined to achieve my goal of trying everything on the menu, I set about shoveling the final few untested delicacies into my mouth. The fact that I had a fifteen hour train journey (followed by a further four hour train journey) provided ample justification for my gluttony.

So, a couple of hours later, with a heavy heart (and stomach) I bid farewell to my friend and her family. I vowed to return soon. Karelia had been a wonderful experience and to date is the most beautiful part of Russia I have been fortunate enough to visit. Despite my sadness, I was excited to start the third and final leg of my summer adventure before a brief visit back to the UK.

# XI.

# Some Observations

## *Security, bureaucracy and buildings*

Having discussed the beauty of Russia in the previous chapter, it is now time to discuss some of the weird and wonderful eccentricities of life here. Please note that the following are merely intended as light-hearted remarks concerning the idiosyncrasies of Russian society. It is these idiosyncrasies to which I have grown accustomed, if not fallen in love with during my short time here.

### *Camouflage, camouflage and more camouflage*

Compared to other capital cities, and in spite of its vast size, Moscow feels like a very safe city. I think this is due to the fact that 99% of its twelve million population work in the field of security. As discussed earlier (Chapter I), when using the metro in Moscow, bag inspections are commonplace. For whatever reason, I seem to be stopped more than most. My American housemate was stopped once during his entire time in Moscow whereas on average I am stopped at least once per week.

## 'WHY ARE YOU GOING THERE?'

Perhaps I simply have the face of a troublemaker. Given the high threat of terrorism, the large presence of security staff here makes perfect sense.

However, you would be severely mistaken if you thought that this was simply a phenomenon of the metro. Security is everywhere here: in supermarkets, shops, banks, museums, car parks and much more. Now, the fact that there is security staff in such places is not strange in itself. Indeed, in England we too have security staff in shops, banks and supermarkets etc. The difference, however, lies in the seriousness, with which people employed in 'security' carry out their job here, often to the point of absurdity. For example, in England, supermarket security officers usually consist of overweight middle aged men or women who, if actually required to chase a thief, would be more likely to suffer a heart attack than to catch the perpetrator running away with a stolen pack of sausage rolls. Yet, in Russia, the supermarket security officer is a force to be reckoned with.

For instance, one afternoon I found myself in a supermarket located on the ground floor of a large shopping centre in the middle of Moscow. As I was at the checkout there was a lady in front of me. She was carrying a plastic bag containing meat which she had evidently bought from a butcher beforehand. As the cashier began to serve this woman she questioned her about the contents of the plastic bag. Apparently not content with her reply, she proceeded to shout 'Okhrana' at the top of her voice. 'Okhrana' (охрана) means 'security'. All of a sudden, out of nowhere, a young woman dressed head to toe in camouflage, came running over to the cashier. The customer and I exchanged a knowing glance, acknowledging the absurdity of the situation. However, before the woman could explain, the security officer dragged her (and her pork chops) away. I never saw her again. I assume that this poor woman is currently locked in a basement being interrogated about where she bought this meat.

## 'WHY ARE YOU GOING THERE?'

*Moscow's business district, known as 'Moscow City'.*

On another occasion, I had the misfortune of visiting 'Moscow City' where I had an appointment. Moscow City is a business area district which comprises of several rather impressive skyscrapers. I see these skyscrapers everyday on my way to the metro. During my walk to the metro I also pass by a traditional Orthodox golden-domed Church. Behind said church you can see Moscow City. The juxtaposition of old and new is visually striking. However, upon actually entering some of the skyscrapers, I was reminded of a documentary on North Korea. In this documentary, the presenter

## 'WHY ARE YOU GOING THERE?'

(Michael Palin) walks around a new airport which, despite being completely empty, is fully staffed for his benefit. Moscow City is similarly eerie. The buildings are huge but completely empty.

Despite the sheer lack of people and businesses, there are security officers everywhere. During my afternoon at Moscow City I managed to get well and truly lost. I found myself entering around four or five different skyscrapers, each of which were identical. Every time I would enter a new building a suited security officer would motion to me to open my rucksack and pass through a metal detector. In a sheer state of confusion, I sometimes entered the same building only for the exact same security officer to again check my bag in the fear that I had perhaps obtained a bomb in the two minutes since we had last met. Sometimes, I even had to pass through security just to enter a different part of the same building. In case you were wondering, I never found the office where my appointment was located and instead simply spent several hours becoming acquainted with Moscow City's security officers.

# 'WHY ARE YOU GOING THERE?'

## *"Passport please"*

A second quirk to which I have had to grow accustomed in Russia is the enormity of bureaucracy necessary to contend with in order to complete the simplest of tasks. I assume (but have no evidence) that this is a hangover from the Soviet Union. I should add that, Russia is not alone in its reputation as a country of red tape. Indeed, Germany is similarly known as a country of bureaucracy. However, in Germany, the bureaucracy seems to be the product of an extremely organised and thorough system which permeates society. Indeed, people often joke about Germans' punctuality and efficiency. In contrast, in Russia, the bureaucracy exists but the reason for such bureaucracy is not always obvious and often feels slightly unnecessary.

For example, one morning, feeling rather flush after payday, I decided to invest in a pair of Bluetooth headphones which I bought online. After paying for the items I could choose to have them delivered or collect them myself. Delivery is notoriously unreliable and unpredictable in Russia and so I decided to collect them myself from an office in the centre of Moscow. Anticipating problems, I made sure to bring my passport. Indeed, in order to enter many buildings it is often required to show your passport.

## 'WHY ARE YOU GOING THERE?'

After eventually finding the correct entrance, I walked up to a man who was sat behind a glass panel. Before I could even explain why I was here he simply said 'Vniz' (вниз) which means 'down' and pointed to a woman downstairs sat behind a similar desk. I gave this woman my passport, from which she wrote my biography. After returning my passport, she provided me with a 'ticket'. I felt like Charlie from *Charlie and the Chocolate Factory*, with my golden ticket. I showed this ticket to the aforementioned man who then proceeded to let me through. I then walked up four flights of stairs before reaching the office from which I was supposed to collect my headphones.

When I reached the office I was met with a sign for a foot massage service. Perplexed, I checked the email on my phone from the company. I had the correct place. I stood there for a few minutes wondering what to do. Eventually, I came to the conclusion that, even if this was a foot massage service, it would not be the end of the world. I had, after all, just walked up four flights of stairs. A foot massage might be nice. I tentatively entered an empty office to be met by a man who was sat behind a desk with his lunch. He grabbed my headphones and, after signing for collection, I was on my way. The man did not offer to massage my feet which was probably for the best. After walking down the same four flights of stairs I handed my golden ticket back to the man behind the desk and I was let free. Even by Russian standards, the whole process required simply to collect a pair of headphones, seemed slightly excessive.

## *"Where is the entrance?"*

As I have already mentioned earlier, it can be extremely difficult to find  buildings in Russia. However, even if you are, in some miraculous feat, able to find the correct building, it is wise not to get too carried away. Finding a building should not be equated with finding the *entrance* of said building. These are two entirely separate challenges. Indeed, on several occasions, I have contemplated smashing a window after exhausting all other options.

For example, as already noted, I recently travelled to the republic of Karelia. I rented an apartment there in a city called Petrozavodsk where I stayed for three weeks. Aside from an abundance of mosquitoes (all of whom took a particular liking to my English blood), Karelia is also well known for its stunning nature. With plenty of time on my hands, I decided to visit a beautiful marble mine park called Ruskeala, as well as an island called Valaam which is home to a monastery. Both of these destinations are difficult to reach independently and so I decided to book an organised tour. Having found a local tour operator I headed off to their office which was allegedly located inside a shopping centre with which I was familiar. Finding the shopping centre was the easy part, now came the small matter of finding how to enter this building and find the office I needed.

With no visible main entrance I circled the building twice before finally settling upon a nondescript door, beyond which I could see a lift. I went through the door and walked into the lift with trepidation. I pressed various buttons in the lift (none of which worked), before swiftly exiting the building, finding myself back where I started. I had noticed a big grey door opposite the lift but nothing about this intimidating big plain door screamed 'entrance'. So, utterly confused, I continued my walk of the perimeter of the building, in search of a more appropriate door.

At this point, I noticed a young woman who also seemed lost. It transpired that she too was looking for a way to enter this impenetrable fortress. As an attempt at a joke, I said to this woman in Russian that I thought that the reason I had been unable to find the entrance was because I was an idiot. She politely smiled but, I couldn't help but notice, said nothing to dismiss the assertion that I was in fact an idiot. Having bonded over our mutual frustration, we entered a nearby restaurant to ask them how to enter the shopping centre.

To my surprise, the entrance was in fact through the aforementioned plain grey door. Once we walked through this door, we then found ourselves in an empty shopping centre. The escalators were covered by sheeting and were clearly not in operation. There were no shops, let alone offices, in sight. However, my eagle eyed companion spotted some stairs which we proceeded to walk up instead. Once I reached the second floor, my companion wished me luck and continued her journey upstairs.

Pleased that I had finally reached my destination, I pulled on the door handle. It was of course locked. After some colourful language, I headed back downstairs, through the grey door and back onto the street. I was defeated. Utterly miserable, I called the local tour operator and explained that I was unable to find their office. With little hesitation, the lady on the phone offered to meet me outside. Something told me that this was not the first time she had done this.

Several minutes later I was warmly greeted by a woman who led me through what looked like a fire exit, past a grim faced security officer and up a flight of stairs to an office which simply had a number on the door and nothing in the way of advertising. I couldn't help but wonder whether this whole episode had actually been some form of test to see whether I had the physical and mental endurance to survive the twelve hour excursion which I was about to book. On the way out of this building, I bumped into my former companion who said congratulations as she walked by, presumingly congratulating me for eventually finding the entrance. This was the first time I had been congratulated for finding the entrance to a building but it was much appreciated.

## *A 'short' walk*

A final thing which I have noticed during my time here is that Russians love walking. In contrast, in England whilst people may go for a short walk to the shops, they do not generally walk for the sake of walking. The only exception to this is Christmas Day afternoon when you are likely to see entire families walking together in an attempt to burn off the thousands of calories they have consumed earlier that day. Thus, even then, the walk is not without purpose.

However, in Russia I often see families and couples hand in hand enjoying an afternoon stroll, particularly during the weekend. Perhaps this should come as no surprise with so many beautiful parks and forests, even in the concrete jungle that is Moscow. Yet, I should add that the term 'walk' takes on an entirely different meaning in Russia. Indeed, an invitation by a Russian acquaintance to join him or her for a walk should be treated with caution. Rather than a leisurely stroll followed by a trip to a cafe, expect instead a three hour hike through forests and areas unknown to civilisation, all of which takes place in subzero temperatures.

Indeed, during my three week adventure in Nizhny Novgorod (see the following chapter), I went on several such 'walks', however one in particular stands out. On the day in question, my peers and I on the university Russian language course had been persuaded by the Russian volunteers on said course to join them for a walk. It was a hot and humid day. After a leisurely stroll around a park we inevitably came to a forest. Now, if in England, this is the point at which I would have turned back. However, our Russian peers assured us that they knew this forest well and we would head through it and it would lead us in the direction of home.

Several hours later we were well and truly lost. The French it seems are even less equipped than the British for such 'walks', as I distinctly remember my French roommate Laurence complaining for the entire journey (this was not completely unjustified). For a while, our Russian friends kept up the pretence that they knew where they were going. However, as the prospect of sleeping under a tree became ever more realistic they finally admitted that we were lost. I had already gathered this from the fact that we had been circling the same forest for several hours. Hot and utterly exhausted, we eventually found our way out of said forest and returned to civilization. The students such as myself were relieved whereas the Russian volunteers did not quite see what all the fuss was about. We had just been on a 'short walk'.

One of the Russian volunteers with whom I became close during my time in Nizhny Novgorod was an attractive and intelligent woman called Valentina. Despite her countless positive attributes, she too is cursed with the Russian understanding of a 'walk'. Indeed, Valentina was one of the 'guides' on the aforementioned ill-fated 'stroll' through the forest. In spite of her questionable navigational skills, I continue to find myself  getting lost with Valentina on so-called 'walks' in areas unknown to civilization. More often than not, these walks last several hours and I find myself shivering in sub-zero temperatures.

During said walks I usually ask her how much further we are going, whining that I am cold and hungry. Her now infamously brutal response is: "until the end". I assume from this phrase that 'the end' refers to the end of the forest or park in which we find ourselves. However, as I clutch at my chest desperately trying to fill my asthmatic lungs with oxygen, it is also conceivable that 'the end', in actual fact refers to the end of my life or, alternatively, the end of time. Coincidentally, both of the latter often seem nearer than the end of the path or forest in which we find ourselves. Thus, based on my above experiences, I would highly advise anyone to proceed with caution before accepting an invitation from a Russian to go on a walk. It may well be your last.

# XII.

## Nizhny Novgorod

### *"Thank you for the beating"*

*The Kremlin of Nizhny Novgorod*

# 'WHY ARE YOU GOING THERE?'

## *Ladybirds and Cockroaches*

After several fantastic (albeit rainy) weeks in Karelia, it was time for my next adventure. I was off to the city of Nizhny Novgorod (Nizhny), the fifth largest city in Russia and one of the host cities for the 2018 FIFA World Cup. I was going to Nizhny to complete a three week Russian language course at the local university. Despite having lived in Russia for eight months, my Russian had not quite improved to the degree of which I would have liked. I felt ready for the challenge, with one exception: the accommodation. When applying for the course, I opted to live in the university dormitory, feeling that this would offer the best experience and enable me to meet my peers.

Yet, when looking on the university website, the price of the dormitory was listed at 1060 roubles (at the time of writing this is just short of £14.00). I assumed that this was a daily rate but I contacted the university just to be sure. To my surprise (and slight horror), this was the price for the entire three weeks of my stay. I would be lying if I said that I wasn't a little anxious regarding my living conditions for the next few weeks. I joked with a friend that perhaps I would be staying on a farm, sharing my bedroom with various cattle.

## 'WHY ARE YOU GOING THERE?'

Thankfully, I was not staying on a farm but rather in a Soviet-style shabby concrete apartment block which was located in the heart of the university campus and was affectionately known as 'Dormitory Number Four'. After locating the building and entrance (this was of course preceded by several failed attempts), I was greeted by the dormitory babushka Tatiana. For those who are not aware, the term 'babushka' generally refers to an elderly Russian woman who, despite her gentle appearance, is a force to be reckoned with. Having survived the trials and tribulations of Communism, she is fearless and demands respect. I had often seen the babushkas of Moscow riding on the metro carrying far more bags than my twenty seven year old 'athletic' physique could ever manage. In fact, one babushka at my local metro station almost knocked me onto the tracks one day as she shoulder barged me out of her way. Needless to say, the Russian babushka is of a different breed to the genteel British grandmother who potters around the city centre before dozing off for a mid afternoon nap at home whilst watching another episode of Noel Edmond's *Deal or No Deal*.

Although I was obviously aware of her ability to make my life a misery for the next three weeks if I disobeyed her, Tatiana seemed delightful. She genuinely seemed pleased to see me and explained that I would be sharing a room with a young French

182

man who knew little Russian but could speak English. She showed me to my room and explained the various rules of the dormitory, the most important of which was the curfew. Tatiana explained that the dormitory closed at eleven o'clock sharp. Should I miss this curfew there was a high probability that I would be sleeping on the street. Summer or not, this did not sound like a pleasant experience.

After being briefed on the rules of the dormitory, Tatiana left me to become acquainted with my new roommate. Laurence was a tall nineteen year old man who was immediately friendly and had a fantastic sense of humour. I instantly knew that we would get on well. After a brief conversation I began to settle into my new surroundings. I had travelled for a total of nineteen hours and was incredibly tired. The room itself seemed fine. We even had a fridge to ourselves which was an unexpected luxury. I was slightly taken aback by the giant ladybirds on my quilt cover but overall I was fairly pleased and reassured with what I had seen. This feeling of reassurance lasted a total of five minutes, after which I ventured into the kitchen and bathroom.

The bathroom was, to put it mildly, atrocious. Often it is easy to pass off old dilapidated buildings as 'Soviet shabby-chic' and, as such, possessing a certain charm. However, there was no charm about this bathroom. There was a pungent smell which emanated from the toilets, explaining the sign requesting that the door be closed after use. In addition, there were no toilet seats nor toilet paper. Should you decide to risk your health by using the toilet facilities you would need to walk down the entire corridor with your own toilet roll in hand. I assume that the refusal to provide communal toilet roll was simply due to a sadistic intention to make the whole process as humiliating as possible. It would have been more subtle to obtain a megaphone and announce to the entire dormitory that I was going for my Monday morning ritual. I tried, wherever possible, to avoid these toilets but regrettably this was not always possible.

On the door of each cubicle there was also a sign asking users not to squat on top of the toilet seats and do their business from a great height. I was told that these signs were aimed at Chinese students who were used to squatting toilets in their own country. I had seen such signs before and had never understood why someone would go to such lengths to complicate what should be a simple process. However, as I looked down at the toilet upon which I was supposed to sit, it suddenly all made sense. In these circumstances, standing on top of the toilet seat and defecating from a great height seemed like the most hygienic option. Regrettably I did not have the leg strength for this.

After my tour of the bathroom, I headed to the communal kitchen which, unfortunately, was not much better. The equipment was old as expected. However, for some inexplicable reason there was also no bin for the rubbish. This meant that people had used all sorts of creative methods to neatly stack their waste inside an empty egg carton. The worst part of this kitchen however was that it was shared. Before I am accused of being snobby and berated for my inability to live in a communal setting, I am not talking about sharing the kitchen with other students. Rather, the kitchen was also shared with a family of cockroaches who had decided to set up home there.

I had the misfortune of meeting the cockroach family on several occasions. Laurence even managed to come across a cremated cockroach inside one of the ovens. I assumed that this was an unfortunate accident and not the forgotten meal of a fellow student. Needless to say, I did not use the kitchen very often.

# 'WHY ARE YOU GOING THERE?'

## *Three Wise Women: The Babushkas of Dormitory Number Four*

In contrast to university accommodation in England where you can come and go as you please, dormitories in Russian universities are staffed by an army of babushkas. There were three babushkas at the dormitory where I stayed, alternating during the week. These babushkas run a tight ship and you cross them at your peril. They have their own room in the dormitory where they sleep and, amongst other things, they are responsible for enforcing the slightly ludicrous eleven o'clock curfew. However, their role extends far beyond this one responsibility. They also act as cleaners, counsellors and general source of wisdom, not to mention doctors.

For example, on one occasion, my roommate announced that he was not feeling particularly well. As we were about to head out for a short walk to the local shop, he was dragged away by the babushka and the director (essentially another, more powerful Babushka) into a room to check his blood pressure. His Russian was limited at this stage so he had no idea what was happening as he gave me a confused wave goodbye. I will be the first to acknowledge the babushka's infinite wisdom. However, at times the medical advice seemed misguided. For example, after checking his blood pressure (which was normal), the babushka told my roommate to rest but at the same time insisted that he drink coffee. As he astutely pointed out to me, resting and caffeine do not often go hand in hand. However, you cannot question the advice of a babushka.

As already mentioned, in total there were three babushkas in charge of the dormitory. The first babushka I met was Tatiana. She was a delightful woman with a great sense of humour and cheerful disposition. She was even nice enough to lie about my artistic 'talent' when I showed her my Christmas bauble which I had lovingly hand painted at a Christmas factory in the middle of July. Regrettably, I do not know the names of the other two babushkas which perhaps speaks volumes. The second babushka was also very friendly but was much quieter than Tatiana and did not seem to have much time for idle chit chat.

Last but not certainly not least, was the third babushka who was positively terrifying. This woman generally viewed us as an inconvenience to her life and ruled the dormitory with an iron fist, particularly when it came to the eleven o'clock curfew. This babushka was perhaps the shortest of the three but what she lacked in height she made up for in personality. Refusing to engage in conversation with us she would simply mutter under her breath. In the entire three weeks, despite my best efforts, I never got her to wish me a good morning. Instead, in response, she would simply mutter 'Mm hmm' with a general disdain for my existence. In fact, one day, towards the end of the course, I wished this babushka a good morning as usual. In response, she asked me when I would be leaving the university which was slightly abrupt even for her.

One Saturday afternoon my roommate and I had discussed the possibility of asking for an extension to the eleven o'clock curfew so that we could experience the nightlife of Nizhny. After plucking up the courage, I knocked on her door and meekly asked her if we could return to the dormitory slightly later this evening. She looked at me with contempt and announced that the dormitory would close at eleven o'clock. There was no room for negotiation. With my tail between my legs, I shuffled out of her room utterly defeated. In response I muttered 'хорошо' (Khorosho) which translates as 'OK' or 'good'. She replied that there had been nothing good about this conversation. I agreed.

As intimidating as she was on this afternoon, this was nothing compared to a few days later when several of us decided to ignore the eleven o'clock curfew and return back to the dormitory late. I had lost track of time in the city centre and found myself with ten minutes to get back to the university which was not possible. As I rushed around I received a text from another girl (Alexandra) from my course who, unaware that I was not there, asked me to tell the babushka that she would be late. This would not be good I thought to myself. I text Laurence, asking him to tell the babushka that both Alexandra and I would be late.

In the end, I was the first to return to the dormitory, little over ten minutes after the curfew. Needless to say, the babushka was frosty with me but no more than usual. Over the next hour, several different groups returned back to the dormitory late and, often, a little worse for wear. Understandably, the babushka began to lose her patience and, unfortunately for her, Alexandra was on the receiving end of this as she returned home an hour late. Despite being tucked up in bed for almost an hour, I heard every terrifying word. I vowed to never return home late again.

# 'WHY ARE YOU GOING THERE?'

## *We wish you a Merry Christmas (In July)*

During our three weeks in Nizhny, the university also sought to show us more about the history and culture of the city. Thus, following language classes in the morning, we would usually have an excursion to various places in the afternoon. One such excursion was to a Christmas factory located in the heart of the city. At this factory they make a variety of Christmas decorations, including beautifully hand painted Christmas baubles.

As impressive as the ornaments were, I will admit that I was not especially excited about this particular excursion for two reasons. Firstly, I hate Christmas. Of course, I haven't always been a Grinch. When I was younger, like every child, I loved Christmas and would wake up early, excited to see what Santa had brought me. However, in recent years, I have started to loathe what is essentially commercialised chaos. I hate the decorations which seem to be put up in city centres earlier and earlier. I hate listening to Wham and Mariah Carey for two months on repeat and I especially hate being told that I should be happy because it is 'Christmas'. If I want to be miserable I should have that choice. The second reason why I was not excited about this excursion was because it was July. There is only one thing worse than

## 'WHY ARE YOU GOING THERE?'

Christmas in December and that is Christmas in July.

After a group photo outside the factory, we entered what was a veritable Christmas wonderland. We were given a tour around the factory and were shown the different stages involved in making the Christmas decorations, from the heating and shaping of the glass to the incredibly detailed hand painting process. It was certainly impressive but nevertheless I was still not feeling very festive. At one point we were taken to a room full of Christmas trees and lights. In the centre of the room was a step upon which we were invited to stand and make a wish. I considered making a wish but in the end I decided against it. Firstly, I doubted that my wish would come true. Secondly, if my wish did come true, there was a real probability that I was going to hell.

After a tour of the factory, it was our turn to get creative. Sat in a large room, we were each provided with a glass bauble and some paint. There was very little else in the way of guidance. Lacking any artistic flair, I did not have particularly high hopes for my work of 'art'. Whilst some of my peers decided to be adventurous, I opted for a simpler design consisting of a Christmas tree and some presents. Half way through I decided to add some colourful spots to my presents. It was downhill from there on. Unfortunately the paint ran and so, improvising, I painted a smiley face on the present instead. It was not my finest hour.

Afterwards, I messaged my mum with a picture of my bauble, insisting that she hang it on the Christmas tree this year. With an equal hatred for Christmas, my mum replied "What tree, I'm not putting one up this year". I don't know whether she had decided this beforehand or whether this was a spontaneous decision taken immediately after viewing my work of art. Following the conclusion of our tour I decided to buy a hand painted bauble in the gift shop for my mum.

### *A Russian Banya: "Thank you for the beating"*

One morning in class my peers were raving about their previous evening at a Banya in the city. A Banya is a Russian sauna where you hit each other with dried birch branches and leaves. Supposedly, the combination of heat and pain (and a stupid hat) is good for your body. Eager to try something new I agreed to join my classmates later that week for what would be an unforgettable experience. On the evening in question one of the Russian volunteers (Valentina) and I were running late so we agreed to meet our friends there. Predictably, this was not as easy as it sounds.

## 'WHY ARE YOU GOING THERE?'

The Banya was located in the basement of an unassuming business centre. Despite being in the same building, I found it necessary to video call my friends who pointed me in the direction of the Banya. After heading downstairs I found myself surrounded by a multitude of industrial grey doors, none of which seemed like the entrance to a sauna. Eventually, my friend met me, opening a door which said 'Exit'. This was the first time that I had had to walk through an 'exit' in order to *enter* a building. However, once inside the Banya, I was impressed. We had the entire Banya to ourselves, consisting of two saunas, an ice pool, showers and dining area. Once we were all together we sat down to enjoy a feast of cheese, pickles, bread and, of course, vodka. It felt like a truly authentic Russian experience.

After stuffing ourselves with food and alcohol, it was time to enter the sauna. Unsure what to expect, I entered with slight trepidation. After enjoying the heat, it was time for some pain. After observing a friend being beaten with a birch plant, I was eager to try this myself. Lying face down, my roommate proceeded to beat me for the next five minutes with an alarming force. Despite also being a first timer, Laurence settled into his role as chief beater with relative ease. At first, he lulled me into a false sense of security by doing something which, in the trade, is known as the 'rainfall'. At this early stage, the assailant soaks the plant in water and then gently sprinkles this over the victim. Just as the victim feels reassured, the assailant proceeds to beat him senseless for several minutes. Afterwards, I jumped into an ice cold pool, ate some food and started the process again. We did this for three hours.

One of my friends announced several days later, that she still had scars from the beating. Due to his exceptional talent, Laurence became the principal beater, with people literally queuing up for a beating. At the end of the evening, one of my friends thanked Laurence for the beating which I thought was extremely polite of her. Laurence replied that he had been happy to help. This was the first time that I had heard someone thank another person for physically abusing them. Returning back to the dormitory, black and blue, I had a feeling that I would sleep well that night.

# 'WHY ARE YOU GOING THERE?'

## *"Alaska is our ice cream"*

In addition to excursions, the university sometimes arranged for us to attend lectures and/or seminars. Again, the idea was to immerse us in not merely the Russian language but also Russian culture. One such lecture was titled *'Russian History: main stages, key events and figures'*. The lecture was given by the Deputy Dean of the Faculty for International Students. As a history buff with a keen interest in the Soviet period, I was particularly interested in this lecture. However, the lecture proved far more interesting than I had imagined.

For the most part, the lecture was uncontroversial. Discussion focused on the origins of Russia and its predecessor known as 'Kyvian Rus'. The adoption of Orthodoxy and the history of the Cyrillic language were also discussed. The lecture was interesting if not mind-blowing. However, the lecture became far more interesting once the lecturer began to discuss the recent and controversial events of late 2013 onwards.

Indeed, in November 2013, protests erupted in the Ukrainian capital of Kyiv. This protest movement became known as 'Euromaidan' after demonstrations erupted in Kyiv's 'Maidan Square' (Independence Square). The protests were triggered by the then President Viktor Yanukovych's decision to pull out of a Free Trade Association Agreement with the European Union in favour of closer ties with Russia. Angry with what many Ukrainians viewed as a betrayal, protests erupted in the capital and turned violent. The protests continued into February 2014 and resulted in a revolution which overthrew the Yanukovych regime. Sadly, many people lost their lives and many more were injured in the process.

Perhaps fearful of the fact that Ukraine now had a pro-European regime, Russia began to get involved in the political situation. The east of Ukraine is home to a large Russian speaking minority. This was used as a pretext for Russian interference. Indeed, between February and March 2014, the Ukrainian peninsula of Crimea was annexed by Russia following a referendum. Crimea had previously belonged to Russia but had been transferred to Ukraine by the Soviet Union in 1954. Many welcomed the return of Crimea to Russia.

However, in the West, the events were seen as an illegal annexation of Ukrainian territory in violation of international law. Furthermore, a full armed conflict erupted in eastern Ukraine between the Ukrainian government and Russian-backed separatist forces. At the time of writing, the conflict continues and people on both sides continue to unnecessarily lose their lives. The eastern regions of

## 'WHY ARE YOU GOING THERE?'

Donetsk and Luhansk have both since declared themselves independent People's Republics.

In light of the above, tensions remain high between Russia and Ukraine. There are currently no direct flights between the countries. As such, when the lecturer announced that he would like to discuss recent events in Ukraine I expected something controversial. I was not disappointed. Discussing the situation in Crimea, he announced that the return of Crimea to Russia reflected the will of the people who lived there and had, in a referendum, voted overwhelmingly to rejoin Russia (the results of the referendum and manner in which it was carried out is contested in the West). He then made the rather bizarre claim that the only reason for American interest in the events was because they wanted Crimea for themselves as a military base.

When discussing the return of Crimea, the lecturer digressed to mention other territories which had formerly belonged to the Russian Empire which, unbeknown to me, included the American territory of Alaska. He explained that there remained some controversy over the deal transferring Alaska to America and that, when questioned about this, Putin once told a reporter that *"Alaska is our ice cream"*. I thought that this was a delightful, if not slightly sinister, quote which perfectly captures the Russian obsession with this cold treat. Indeed, Russians love ice cream. I once saw a woman tucking into an ice cream on the metro at 8.30am on a weekday morning which I thought was slightly excessive.

However, this quote attributed to Putin was not the only highlight of this lecture. When discussing the protests in Kyiv, he announced that those involved were foreign agents paid by the West to destabilize the situation in Ukraine. How else could people afford to stop work and protest? It was apparently unfathomable that individuals would stop work and join a protest movement relating to the future direction of their country. Next, the lecturer announced that Mikhail Gorbachev, the final leader of the Soviet Union, and a man praised in the West for ending the Cold War, was also a spy. I found this a rather bold claim. However, Laurence has since shown me an advert in which Gorbachev appeared for Pizza Hut in the late nineties which seems to support this claim. After watching this advert it seems hard to escape the conclusion that Gorbachev was a spy paid by Western fast food outlets to destroy the Soviet Union and bring pizza to Russia.

Last but not certainly not least, the same lecturer announced that, in his view, Joseph Stalin was the best leader of the Soviet Union. He based this assertion on Stalin's achievement in transforming an agrarian country into a huge industrial power in such a short period of time. I found this comment particularly distasteful. Whilst Stalin did indeed industrialise the country, this overlooks the fact that he was a brutal dictator who was responsible for the death of millions. To call him a good leader is an insult to his victims.

Nonetheless, sadly, our lecturer is not alone in his views. Russia continues to have a confusing attitude towards Stalin which is reflected by the fact that he remains buried by the Kremlin Wall in the heart of Moscow. In his conclusion, our lecturer announced that what he had discussed was not propaganda but fact. Despite my opposing views, the lecture had been nothing if not interesting.

### *Christmas baubles and trains*

Eventually, the day had come for me to leave Nizhny Novgorod and head back to Moscow for the weekend before flying back to London. I will admit that I was rather sad to leave. I had spent a wonderful three weeks in what is a beautiful city with some amazing people. I vowed to return soon. Whether my Russian had improved the extent to which I had hoped was debatable. Nevertheless, it had been a truly memorable experience.

## 'WHY ARE YOU GOING THERE?'

However, even on this final warm summer day, I remained haunted by the spectre of Christmas. Despite now being somewhat of a packing expert, I was unable to find space to pack my two Christmas baubles in my suitcase. I considered throwing them into the River Volga but realised that it would be difficult to achieve this from the taxi window as it hurtled towards the train station. Instead, my favourite babushka, Tatiana, provided me with a carrier bag from a cosmetics shop which I used to carry them. This prevented me from 'forgetting' said baubles in the dormitory.

# 'WHY ARE YOU GOING THERE?'

# XIII.

# A Complicated History

## *The legacy of Communism in Russia*

*A statue of Vladimir Lenin in Petrozavodsk, Karelia*

## 'WHY ARE YOU GOING THERE?'

During the 2013-2014 Euromaidan Revolution, angry Ukrainian protesters were seen violently toppling a giant statue of Vladimir Lenin which was housed on Kiev's main Khreshchatyk Street **(8)**. For protestors, this statue of the Russian father of Communism represented decades of Russian oppression and marked a pivotal moment in Ukraine's transition towards becoming a truly independent country in the post-Soviet world. By contrast, in Moscow alone there are eighty statues of Vladimir Lenin, not to mention throughout the rest of Russia **(9)**. It is also worth noting that the man himself remains embalmed in a mausoleum in the heart of Moscow that is Red Square.

It may seem that the presence of a statue of a now deceased leader, built several decades ago in a country which no longer exists has little to no impact on modern-day society. To an extent this is true. However, to a larger extent, the very refusal to topple such statues, in stark contrast to Russia's post-Soviet neighbours, in fact speaks volumes. It serves as evidence of a country with a complicated history: a history with which is still struggles to grapple.

Despite my short time in Russia, I have noticed a confusing attitude of Russians towards their own history which is sometimes baffling for an outsider to understand. It is this legacy of communism in a post-Soviet Russia to which I now turn. However, I should add that, the following only constitutes a brief insight into the legacy of communism in modern-day Russia based on my own personal experiences and observations. For those interested in reading further about the legacy of Communism in the post-Soviet world, I would highly recommend the excellent work of Belarusian author Svetlana Alexeivich **(10)**.

## *Lenin and Stalin: Good vs. Evil?*

When people think of Communism and the Soviet Union, two names immediately come to mind: Vladimir Lenin and Joseph Stalin. Vladimir Lenin, born in 1870, was the leader of the Bolshevik Party which triumphed in the October 1917 revolution, successfully overthrowing the Tsarist regime and installing a communist government based upon the principles of Marxism. Following the revolution, Lenin served as the head of Soviet Russia from 1917 until his death in 1924. His successor, Joseph Stalin, a Georgian by birth, served as head of the Soviet Union from 1924 until his death in 1953. Both men played a key role in the creation and maintenance of the 'worker's paradise' State that was the Soviet Union. However, the way in which these two men are viewed in modern Russia couldn't be more different.

## 'WHY ARE YOU GOING THERE?'

In short, Lenin is largely viewed as the 'good' Marxist revolutionary who sought to create a classless State based on socialist ideas. On the other hand, Stalin is viewed (and rightfully so) as a tyrant responsible for the death of millions of innocent people. However, in modern Russia, things are often not as they seem and, in reality, the legacy of these two men nowadays is much more complicated.

Indeed, as someone who has visited several former eastern bloc countries, one thing which is striking about Russia in comparison to those countries, is the continued presence of Lenin. As already noted, in the former eastern bloc countries, the installation of a democratic regime was swiftly followed by an avid decommunisation. More recently, Ukraine even went as far as adopting 'decommunisation' laws, which *inter alia*, ban Communist symbols **(11)**. With the fall of the Iron Curtain, statues of Lenin and other Soviet heroes were hurriedly torn down as a testament to liberalisation from Russian oppression. Some were simply demolished whilst others were moved and are now part of outdoor exhibitions. Noteworthy examples of such exhibitions include Muzeon Park of Arts in Moscow and the fascinating Memento Park in Budapest.

## 'WHY ARE YOU GOING THERE?'

In contrast, Vladimir Lenin remains noticeably present not just in Moscow but throughout Russia. In the five cities which I have been fortunate to visit to date, each has at least one looming statue of Lenin and is usually accompanied by a main street named after him. In addition, as already noted, Vladimir Lenin remains embalmed in a mausoleum on Red Square which is open to the public and remains a popular tourist attraction. One afternoon I visited this mausoleum. I would recommend curious tourists to also visit but would hasten to add that it all feels very surreal and eerie, with Lenin looking less and less human as the years pass by.

Once you enter the mausoleum it is dark and cold but most noticeably, silent. Visiting Lenin is treated as a very serious and somber affair with staff shushing a pair of Chinese tourists in front of me upon entering the mausoleum. At particularly busy times you are permitted to do a brief walk around the perimeter of the room in silence before being hurried out. In recent years there have been calls for Lenin to be removed from Red Square and buried but, despite this, he remains on Red Square for the foreseeable future.

# 'WHY ARE YOU GOING THERE?'

On the other hand, former Soviet leader Joseph Stalin is viewed rather differently than his predecessor. In modern-day Russia you will struggle to find a statue of Joseph Stalin. The reason for this is that, following his death in 1953, the Soviet authorities, led by Nikita Krushchev, embarked on a policy of de-Stalinization in an attempt to wipe out any traces of his existence. Although this is not something I have felt appropriate to discuss with Russians during my time here (I generally avoid conversations about politics or other controversial issues), I would argue that a large number of Russians regard Stalin as a bloodthirsty dictator responsible for the death of millions.

However, even if this is the case, his legacy remains somewhat ambiguous. In recent years, statues commemorating Stalin have been constructed in Russia **(12)**. Nevertheless, most shocking of all is the fact that, once you exit Lenin's mausoleum you will come face to face with a statue of Stalin, denoting the burial place of one of the most brutal dictators the world has ever known. The fact that he remains buried in the heart of Moscow is baffling and, in my view, an insult to the millions of victims who perished under his regime.

# 'WHY ARE YOU GOING THERE?'

## *Architecture: Skyscrapers and Sickles*

Excepting the countless statues and streets named after Lenin, perhaps the most prominent physical reminder of Russia's complicated history is its architecture. Moscow, in particular, is littered with buildings which range from the imposing Stalinist skyscrapers to the low-rise concrete apartment buildings known as 'Khrushchyovkas' named after Stalin's successor, Nikita Krushchev. Often nestled in between these buildings are magnificent gleaming gold-domed churches. It is such varying architectural styles which make Moscow such a wonderful place to live. At every turn there is a surprise for your eyes which are guaranteed to never get bored. I should add that many of the beautiful churches, despite their seemingly ancient appearance, are in fact reconstructions. This is true in particular of my favourite cathedral in Moscow, a white cathedral with golden domes known as the cathedral of Christ the Saviour. This cathedral was demolished by the Soviet authorities in December 1931 and was transformed into the world's largest open-air swimming pool **(13)**. It was not rebuilt to its former glory until the beginning of the twenty first century.

## 'WHY ARE YOU GOING THERE?'

In terms of remaining Stalinist architecture, there are seven main skyscrapers in Moscow which have affectionately been dubbed 'Stalin's Seven Sisters'. This is a collection of seven imposing skyscrapers which were built under the Stalin regime between the years of 1947 and 1953. They include: Hotel Ukraina (now Radisson Hotel), Kotelnicheskaya Embankment Apartments, the Kudrinskaya Square Building, the Hilton Moscow Leningradskaya Hotel, the main building of the Ministry of Foreign Affairs, the main building of Moscow State University and the Red Gates Administrative Building (2). I have been fortunate enough to visit three of Stalin's sisters to date, namely: Hotel Ukraina (remember my eventful evening with a Russian model, discussed in Chapter VII?), Leningradskaya Hotel and the Kotelnicheskaya Embankment Apartments, the ground floor of which is home to a rather wonderful small cinema named 'Illusion'. I will make an effort to visit Stalin's other sisters in the near future.

It is worth nothing that the common perception in the West is that Russia and, indeed, the former eastern bloc countries, are rather grey and dreary places comprising solely of grey concrete high-rise buildings to match the equally dreary grey skies. To a certain extent this cannot be denied. Indeed, as already noted, Moscow is well known (and rightly so) for being a concrete jungle. In addition, the weather here is often as brutal as its architecture. At the time of writing (December), I cannot remember the last time I have seen the sun or indeed a blue sky. Nevertheless, this is only half of the picture. Moscow is in fact also a very green city with a total of five hundred and fifty parks and trees and shrubs covering forty nine percent of the city's area **(14)**. Indeed, in summer, with the sun shining and a multitude of outdoor cafes, Moscow feels like any other cosmopolitan European city.

Last but not least, a discussion of Moscow's architecture would be wholly incomplete without a brief comment on its metro system which, I must re-emphasise is absolutely stunning and a work of art in its own right. A project of Stalin who demanded that metro stations be designed as 'palaces of the people', they are unlike anything else I have seen and well worth a visit. With an earlier chapter dedicated entirely to the Moscow Metro, it is unnecessary to go into further detail here.

# 'WHY ARE YOU GOING THERE?'

## *Hangovers from the Soviet Period*

In addition to the visible reminders of Russia's Communist past noted above, I have also noticed some more subtle reminders, so-called 'hangovers' from the Soviet period. In contrast to the above, these 'hangovers' primarily relate to a certain mentality or traits which I have observed living in modern Russian society. It is these to which I now turn.

Firstly, one thing which I have noticed during my time here is a specific and distinct attitude towards work, compared to the West. Indeed, one thing I have observed is the excessive workforce often employed for what seems to be a rather simple task. For example, it is common when using the metro to find that one of the escalators is broken and in the process of being repaired. This often takes several months. Although these escalators are notoriously long, to my mind (and I stress that I am no expert in the field of escalator repair) two to three staff at most should be sufficient to complete this task. However, I have often witnessed five or even six members of staff standing around the same escalator in dismay. Despite this workforce, the repair still takes several months. On a related note, I have been told first-hand from Russian friends that they sometimes turn up to work and find that they have nothing to do. Or, they finish their tasks for the day earlier but are unable to leave the office earlier accordingly because those are the rules. Work hours are fixed irrespective of employees' workload or productivity.

Whilst I have no evidence to support this, I believe that this current attitude towards work is a continuing hangover from the Soviet period. The Soviet Union was designed as a 'Worker's Paradise' where everyone was provided with a job. There was an undeniable job security. Indeed, this is one of the things lamented today by those who experienced life in the Soviet Union, namely the resulting lack of job security in the new Post-Soviet Russia. However, whilst the Soviet government was proud of its record with regards to providing work, the reality is that this came at a cost: productivity. A planned economy does not take into account the supply and demand of the market meaning that hugely staffed State enterprises were often wholly unproductive and unprofitable. The Soviet economic model was unsustainable and was one of many factors responsible for the collapse of the Soviet Union. There have of course been many changes since those times but, in my opinion, the attitude towards work in modern-Russia seems to be a direct hangover from that period.

## 'WHY ARE YOU GOING THERE?'

There are however some more positive hangovers from the Soviet Union in current Russian society which I have observed and are equally worthy of note. For example, during the Soviet Union a strong emphasis was placed on the arts, including the theatre. It is undeniable that the theatre, as with all forms of art, was used by the Soviet government as a propaganda tool and was only permitted to the extent that it was in alignment with the values of 'social realism'. However, this aside, it is undeniable that a major achievement of the Soviet authorities was to make the arts accessible to all.

To this day, the theatre remains extremely accessible and of superb quality. When living in England I rarely visited the theatre due to it being relatively expensive. Unless you have a comfortable salary, it is not something which you can afford to do on a regular basis. In contrast, in Moscow you will readily find tickets for the theatre for under £10. For my birthday I watched an impressive performance of Dostoevsky's *Crime and Punishment* at a theatre in central Moscow for less than £10. The continuing accessibility of the arts seems to be a direct consequence of the emphasis placed on this industry by the Soviet authorities.

## 'WHY ARE YOU GOING THERE?'

A final hangover from the Soviet period which I have noticed during my time here is that, in comparison to the West, Russian society remains much more communitarian and less focused on the individual. Compared to the UK, Russian people seem much more willing and eager to help one another. For example, it is commonplace when using the metro to see gentlemen offering to help women with pushchairs or to help carry the bags of elderly women.

In addition, whenever I have dropped anything on the floor (which happens much more often than is acceptable) people are quick to point this to my attention. As already noted, it is also etiquette to give up your seat on the metro for the elderly. All of the above are indications of what thoroughly remains a communitarian society. I am not of course saying that such behaviour does not exist elsewhere such as the UK but, to my mind, it happens to a much lesser extent.

Again, whilst I have no evidence to support this, I firmly believe that this emphasis on the community rather than the individual is another hangover from the Soviet period. During the times of the Soviet Union everyone was working towards a common goal, namely the creation of a worker's utopia and of a society fair and just for all. Rather than the needs and wants of the individual, focus was very much on the greater good and the needs of the community. This focus on the community rather than the individual remains in modern day Russia and is something which should be celebrated.

### *Religion in modern-day Russia*

Last, but certainly not least, a few comments ought to be made on the status of religion in modern-day Russia. Indeed, current attitudes towards religion are a direct consequence of the sustained attack on the church committed by the Soviet authorities during the Communist period. This has led to a somewhat confusing attitude towards religion and an even more complicated relationship between the Church and the State.

The success of the October 1917 Revolution, and subsequent installation of a Communist government, marked the beginning of a long and sustained attack on religion in the Soviet Union. There was no place or need for religion in a Communist society. The New Faith was that of socialism. Any other faith was redundant. Indeed, Vladimir Lenin compared religion to a venerable disease **(15)**. The Soviet State subsequent sought to eliminate religion, with efforts redoubled during Stalin's tenure **(15)**. Thousands of clergy were killed during Stalin's purges of 1936 and 1937 **(15)**. As already noted, many churches, including the striking cathedral of Christ the Saviour, were destroyed and not rebuilt until the collapse of the Soviet Union. The celebration of Christmas (which takes place on 07 January in accordance with the Orthodox calendar) was even banned, with emphasis instead being placed on New Year **(16)**.

Indeed, it is unfathomable that such a brutal and sustained attack would not have an impact on the status of religion for decades to come. In my opinion, and based on my observations, despite an abundance of churches, the number of practicing Christians in modern-day Russia is less than in pre-Revolutionary Russia. Whilst the celebration of Christmas Day is no longer outlawed (and even constitutes a public holiday), it remains significantly overshadowed by New Year celebrations **(16)**. What we in the West refer to as a Christmas Tree continues to be termed a 'New Year Tree' in modern Russia. Indeed, whilst the physical destruction of the church can be redressed, the mental scars remain.

The confusing state of religion in modern Russia was epitomised for me one day when visiting a church in Petrozavodsk. One summer afternoon, I entered said church and, as usual, found myself mesmerised by the beautiful icons and gold decoration. It was at this point that I looked across the room to see a man walking around the church and crossing himself. At the same time, he was wearing a red t-shirt with the abbreviation 'CCCP' spread across his chest, complete with hammer and sickle. I seemed to be alone in acknowledging the irony of a man who, I have no doubt, considers himself a devout Christian, wearing a T-shirt commemorating the very State which did everything in its power to destroy the Christian faith.

Finally, it is worth commenting upon the somewhat peculiar relationship which currently exists between the Russian State and the Orthodox church. According to the 1993 Constitution, Russia is a secular State **(17)**. However, despite this, some have questioned the current relationship between the Church and State. This issue was subtly addressed by the renowned director Andrey Zyagintsev in his compelling 2014 film *Leviathan*. This tells the story of one man's battle to prevent his house from being seized by a corrupt mayor. The film ends with a shot of the land where the man's house used to be. In its place was a large golden-domed church.

This film is not so far from reality. Indeed, there is currently a close relationship between the Church and the State in Russia. This arguably fits in with the goal of creating a national identity and unity (which often also seems to result in a nationalism which pits Russia against the West). However, in a sign that perhaps Russian society is fighting back against this close relationship between Church and State, protesters in the city of Yekaterinburg, recently successfully halted the construction of a Church in a famous square **(18)**. However, truthfully, these protests were as much about the construction of a church as they were about local democracy and citizens' involvement in decision-making **(18)**.

In summary, despite the Soviet Union collapsing more than more than twenty years ago, its legacy very much lives on in modern-day Russia. It lives on in statues, in architecture but also in peoples' minds. This is a society which continues to grapple with its complicated history and find its way in a new, capitalist era. With the existence of a Communist state for more than seventy years, it is foolish to believe that its legacy would be extinguished in a mere twenty or thirty years.

# 'WHY ARE YOU GOING THERE?'

# XIV.

# A Brief Interlude

## *Coming Home or Going Home?*

"Excuse me, do you know where carriage C is?", I asked a young woman as I stood opposite my train at London's St Pancras train station. "I don't have a *bloody* clue", she replied, in an unmistakable East Midlands accent. It was July and I hadn't heard this accent for eight months. It was warm and friendly and reminded me that I was home. Confused, I waited until, eventually, the carriage numbers were displayed. I boarded the train, ready for the final leg of my journey: a two hour train journey back to my hometown of Derby. After storing my rather large and battered suitcase in the luggage compartment I wearily settled into my seat.

It had been a long day. I had woken up at six o'clock that morning and headed to Moscow's Sheremetyevo airport to board a flight to Heathrow. Despite arriving at Heathrow at midday I had opted to book an evening train. It felt like a good idea at the time. I had a friend who had recently moved to London and I thought this would be a good opportunity to catch up. However, seven hours in

## 'WHY ARE YOU GOING THERE?'

London with a suitcase in tow had taken it out of me. An earlier indication of my fatigue had taken place at lunchtime. Dining at a popular Italian restaurant in Covent Garden, I thanked my waitress as she brought my order over. Of course, thanking a waitress for your food is not, in itself, a sign of fatigue. However, the problem was that I had thanked her in perfect Russian. Confused, she smiled awkwardly and briskly walked off.

So, after a long and tiring day, I was ready to get home. I closed my eyes as the tannoy onboard reverberated throughout the train: "Good evening, ladies and gentlemen, I would just like to apologise again (this was already the second time the lady on the tannoy had apologised) for the fact that this evening's train has fewer carriages than expected. I can see that you are helping each other which is appreciated. I will make my way through the train shortly to assist further. Sorry for any inconvenience. Thank you."

I looked around the train. Everyone I could see had a seat and no one seemed to be taking any interest in the announcement. "What inconvenience?", I thought to myself. A second apology seemed excessive. I closed my eyes again and tried to imagine the same apology being repeated onboard a Russian train. I couldn't. The frequent use of the word 'sorry', even for the mildest of misdemeanors, was another reminder that I was home.

More than half way through my journey, I opened my rucksack to obtain my phone charger as my battery was running low. I removed the carrier bag containing my Christmas baubles from Nizhny Novgorod. As I did so, I couldn't help but hear a faint jingle. After dismissing my initial fears that this was perhaps the sound of Santa's sleigh, I understood that the inevitable had happened. Sure enough, as I peeked inside the bag I saw nothing but shards of glass. Further inspection revealed that it was of course the professional and beautifully painted bauble which I had bought in the shop which had broken into smithereens. Regrettably my own lackluster effort had survived. I doubted whether a grenade could blow apart this robust work of 'art'.

An hour later, I knocked on the door of my mum's house. I decided to get the gift-giving out the way immediately handing her my carrier bag of broken glass. Perhaps as an indication of how much she had missed me, she still allowed me to come inside. This was in spite of the fact that after eight months abroad, my only gift was essentially a weapon. Such is a mother's love.

## 'WHY ARE YOU GOING THERE?'

I spent the next five weeks living with my mum and sister in my childhood home. Aside from some arguments, the type of which are inevitable when three adults are living together in close proximity, everything was perfect and I enjoyed a much needed break. During these three weeks I was also fortunate enough to attend my sister's wedding in Italy. As much as I enjoyed this time away from my new home, near the end of my time in England I found myself itching to get back to my new life as the academic year approached. As I boarded the flight at Heathrow back to Moscow it was hard to escape the feeling that I was going home as opposed to leaving home.

# XV.

# Conclusion

## *One Year Later*

As I sit here in my mother's living room, surrounded by Christmas decorations, I realise that it has almost been one year since I decided to pack up my life and move to Russia. I can honestly say that this was the best decision of my life and has opened my eyes to a new world, a new culture and a new way of life. I look forward to continuing this journey, wherever it may take me. With the year coming to a close, now is perhaps the perfect time to reflect upon the unsurprisingly large differences between England and Russia. However, rather than bore you with long and detailed ruminations, I thought it would be better to instead write a short list of things which I miss about England, followed by the same list with regards to Russia. I will start with the former.

# 'WHY ARE YOU GOING THERE?'

## *A short list of things which I miss about England*

Without further ado, here is a short list of things which I miss about England, having lived in Russia for the past year:

1. *Family*
2. *Friends*
3. *Curry* (I am yet to find good spicy food in Russia).
4. *A Sunday Roast*
5. *The word 'sorry'*
6. *Talking about the weather*
7. *Talking about Brexit*
8. *Smiling at strangers*
9. *A cup of tea with milk*
10. *British Comedy*

The above is merely a short list of things which I miss about living in England. These are the first things which come to mind and should not be regarded as a complete list. I also hasten to add that, despite their numberings, it should not be assumed that the list reflects any form of ranking system. It is arguable that I have missed a curry more than my family and friends. That is of course a joke. I think. Although, I really have missed a curry.

# 'WHY ARE YOU GOING THERE?'

## *A short list of things which I miss about Russia*

Having lived in Russia for the past twelve months, there are certain things to which I have become accustomed and even grown to like. These are as follows:

1. *Friends and colleagues*
2. *Snow (Russia in winter is beautiful)*
3. *Borscht (or in fact any soup)*
4. *Georgian food*
5. *Not saying 'sorry' (not feeling the need to say 'sorry' when someone bumps into you is a refreshing and unfamiliar feeling for a Brit).*
6. *Not talking about the weather*
7. *Not talking about Brexit*
8. *Babushkas*
9. *The Moscow Metro*
10. *Streets named after Lenin*

Similarly to the first list, this list is also, in all likelihood, incomplete, and should not be regarded as being in any particular order.

# 'WHY ARE YOU GOING THERE?'

## *Going home?*

In just over one week, I will be flying back to Moscow, ready to start a new year in Russia. My current contract (which commenced in September) is for nine months, guaranteeing that I will at least be residing in Moscow until next summer. I have been asked several times in England whether I have moved to Russia permanently and I find myself unable to answer this question. Whilst the prospect of living in Russia for the rest of my life seems far-fetched, I am in no rush to leave. Against all obstacles (particularly the complexity of the Russian language), I find myself surprisingly settled and content in my new life. As cliché as it sounds, when I board the plane back to Moscow in a few days, I have a suspicion that I will feel as if I am *going* home rather than *leaving* home. Of course, having spent twenty seven years here, England will always be my home. Nevertheless, Russia is home *right now*.

# 'WHY ARE YOU GOING THERE?'

## *On a more serious note*

My aim when commencing writing on this book was to provide a humorous, tongue-in-cheek account of life in Russia for a British expat. I hope that I have achieved this aim. The majority of this book has focused on the funny, strange and sometimes downright bizarre things which have happened to me. I should hasten to add that everything which I have written is true. Sometimes the truth is indeed stranger than fiction. However, on the (perhaps misguided) assumption, that I have achieved the aforementioned aim, I would like to end this book on a more serious note which I feel is only fitting.

As you may remember from the Prologue, I received a variety of different reactions from people in England upon hearing that I was moving to Russia. These ranged from mild curiosity to wild disbelief and warnings regarding impending arrest. I am pleased to report that, as I write this, I am safe and well and have so far escaped the attention of the KGB's successor the FSB. When watching the news in England (and undoubtedly in other Western European countries), it often paints a bleak picture of Russia. A failing economy crippled by sanctions and an authoritarian regime which brutally silences its critics.

## 'WHY ARE YOU GOING THERE?'

However, what I lament is that, in light of the news, people are often unable to separate a regime from its people and culture thus, refuse to visit a country. There are indeed certain countries where, in my opinion, the political and human rights situation are such, that it would be morally wrong to visit and provide hard currency to the regime (North Korea comes to mind). However, aside from these extreme examples, I would urge people not to be put off from visiting a country solely due to negative news stories. In particular, I would urge people to visit the beautiful and fascinating country that is Russia.

In the last twelve months I have been fortunate enough to wander across a snowy Red Square, see Lenin, admire the beautiful and picturesque nature of Karelia, and stroll alongside the ancient Kremlin walls of Nizhny Novgorod. Russia is a breathtaking and captivating country with a wonderful culture and generous and hospitable people. So far, I have only visited the Western, European half of the country. There is much more to see. So, if I could offer any final advice, it would be to put aside the bleak news stories which you might have read and to come visit this remarkable country.

## 'WHY ARE YOU GOING THERE?'

*"Why are you going there?"*

The title of this book is *"Why are you going there?"*. This was a question I was often asked by people in England who were confused upon hearing my news. I hope that this book provides a comprehensive response. However, upon reflection, perhaps this book, subconsciously, was as much a response to myself as it was to those who were confused by my choice.

Twelve months ago, I was working as an immigration lawyer, surrounded by friends and family, living in my hometown where I had spent the majority of my life. I had never know anything different. Having made such a monumental life change, perhaps I needed to answer this question to myself as a reassurance that I had made the right choice. As a result of the previous year, I am a happier, more confident and, I would like to think, a more rounded individual. Thus, upon reflection, I feel that I am now finally in a position to properly answer the question which serves as the title of this book.

# 'WHY ARE YOU GOING THERE?'

# Acknowledgements

I am grateful to many people who have read and commented upon this book, thereby helping me to create this body of work of which I am immensely proud. I would like to thank my former colleagues as well as my friends (both in the UK and Russia). Their comments and advice were invaluable. However, particular gratitude is extended to my friend and mentor Mr. Peter Dawson OBE and his wife Shirley Dawson who have supported this endeavour from the beginning and have been a consistent source of support. Without such support, none of this would have been possible.

# References

**(1)** *The Guardian, 'Dozens injured after Georgia police fire rubber bullets at demonstrators'*: https://www.theguardian.com/world/2019/jun/20/georgian-police-teargas-crowd-russian-lawmaker-parliament (21 June 2019)

**(2)** Wikipedia, *'Seven Sisters (Moscow)*: https://en.wikipedia.org/wiki/Seven_Sisters_(Moscow)

**(3)** *'История создания Московского Метро'* (*'History of the creation of the Moscow Metro'*) (in Russian): https://web.archive.org/web/20010420031732/http://sachak.chat.ru/istoria.html
Also see: http://news.metro.ru/letopis.html

**(4)** Wikipedia, *'Moscow Metro'*: https://en.wikipedia.org/wiki/Moscow_Metro#First_four_stages_of_construction

**(5)** France 24, *'Moscow's help for the homeless expands 'out of sight'* (27 February 2019) https://www.france24.com/en/20190227-moscows-help-homeless-expands-out-sight

**(6)** Wikipedia, *'Ploschad Revolyutsii (Moscow Metro)'*: https://en.wikipedia.org/wiki/Ploshchad_Revolyutsii_(Moscow_Metro)#cite_note-2

# 'WHY ARE YOU GOING THERE?'

**(7)** Wikipedia, *'Mayakovskaya (Moscow Metro)'*:
https://en.wikipedia.org/wiki/Mayakovskaya_(Moscow_
Metro)

**(8)** The Guardian, *'Kiev protesters topple Lenin statue as
protesters take to the street'* (08 December 2013):
https://www.theguardian.com/world/2013/dec/08/kiev-
protesters-lenin-statue-ukraine

**(9)** Culture Trip, *'Where Have Russia's Lenin Statues
Gone?'* (08 May 2018):
https://theculturetrip.com/europe/russia/articles/where-
have-russias-lenin-statues-gone/

**(10)** In particular, I would highly recommend Svetlana
Alexeivich's book *Second-hand Time* (Fitzcarraldo
Editions, 5 May 2016).

**(11)** *The Guardian, 'Ukraine to rewrite Soviet history
with controversial 'decommunisation' laws'* (20 April
2015):
https://www.theguardian.com/world/2015/apr/20/ukraine
-decommunisation-law-soviet

**(12)** *The Atlantic, 'Is Stalin Making a Comeback in
Russia?' (28 May 2019)*:
https://www.theatlantic.com/international/archive/2019/0
5/russia-stalin-statue/590140/

# 'WHY ARE YOU GOING THERE?'

**(13)** For more information see: *"Храм Христа Спасителя"*:
http://new.xxc.ru/about/kompleks_hrama/hram_hrista_sp asitelya/

**(14)** Moscow Mayor Official Website, '*Moscow Key Performance Indicators*':
https://www.mos.ru/en/city/projects/development/

**(15)** The Guardian, '*Why the Soviet attempt to stamp out religion failed*' (26 October 2017):
https://www.theguardian.com/commentisfree/belief/2017/oct/26/why-the-soviet-attempt-to-stamp-out-religion-failed

**(16)** The Independent, '*Orthodox Christmas: When does Russia celebrate it and why is the date different around the world?*' (06 January 2017):
https://independent.co.uk/life-style/orthodox-christmas-when-why-how-russia-celebrate-date-14-january-greek-greece-catholic-church-a7512666.html

**(17)** 'Text of the Russian constitution in English' (Constituteproject.org) (see Article 13(1): *'No ideology shall be proclaimed as State ideology or as obligatory'.*

**(18)** Radio Free Europe/ Radio Liberty, '*Church of Strife: Construction Plans Divide Russia's Fourth-Largest City*' (17 May 2019):
https://www.rferl.org/amp/29947842.html

Printed in Great Britain
by Amazon